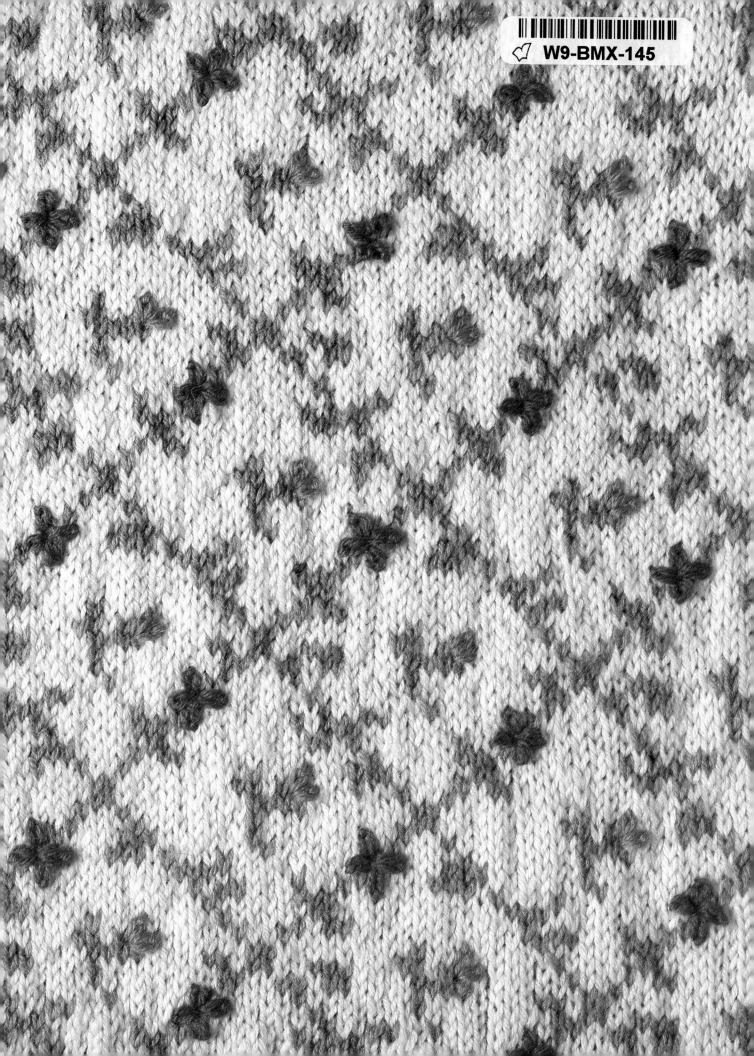

THE
BEATRIX POTTER
KNITTING BOOK

*For my husband and my two dear daughters who endured my disappearance
for many hours at a time while I was producing this book;
also with love and gratitude for my late mother who gave me so much
and for Betty Tullis to whom I owe my career*

Facing page: Flopsy Bunnies Baby's Jumper (page 53)

THE
BEATRIX POTTER
KNITTING BOOK

PAT MENCHINI

Photography by Tony Boase

F. WARNE & Co

I wish to thank the National Trust, who so kindly allowed Hill Top, Sawrey, and High Tilberthwaite Farm, Coniston, to be used in connection with many of the garments photographed in this book. In addition, I would like to extend my personal thanks to Dr and Mrs Kellgren for the use of their beautiful home and garden.

My special thanks go to Tony Boase for his wonderful photography and to Sue Terry for her clever styling and continued support from the first moment the book was conceived. I also wish to thank the owners of Grizedale Lodge Hotel, Hawkshead, for their warmth and hospitality while the book was being photographed.

In addition, the book would not have been possible without the help of all those manufacturers whose yarns and embroidery threads are featured. Their assistance has been of great help and I extend my warmest thanks. Also, my thanks go to Jenny Laycock for her clever interpretation of my rug ideas.

Not least, a word about the superb band of ladies scattered all over England and Scotland, many of whom I have never met, who through many faithful years of knitting, sewing, technical checking and typing for me have become part of my life. Without them this book would never have been possible – my thanks to you all!

PAT MENCHINI

The author and publishers would like to thank the following for their assistance:

Viyella, Country Casuals, Dickins & Jones, New Man and *Laura Ashley* for the model girl's accessories. *Bally* for her shoes. *Charnos* for tights. *Mothercare* for the children's accessories and tights, and the pram, cot and Moses basket. *Start-Rite* for the children's shoes. *Anello & Davide* for ballet shoes. *Cornelia James* for gloves and scarves. *Dickins & Jones* for jewellery. *Daisy Chain* of Cambridge for beaded hair-combs, earrings, pearl and flower rope and green and brown beaded chunky necklace. *Viyella* for plain white, pink and patterned fabric. *Gordon Thoday* of Cambridge for the cotton broderie anglais and black moire fabric. *Bodgers* of Cambridge for the boater, cap, tweed hat, woollen stockings and cravat. *Marks & Spencer* for the man and older boy's accessories. *Copyrights* for the Beatrix Potter wallpaper, fabric, pictures and soft toys. *Sanderson* for the 'Chatsworth' curtain fabric. *S. Warwick & Son* of Cambridge for the tapestry firescreen frame and stand. *Fulton* for the umbrella.

FREDERICK WARNE
Published by the Penguin Group
27 Wrights Lane, London W8 5TZ, England
Viking Penguin Inc., 40 West 23rd Street, New York, New York 10010, USA
Penguin Books Australia Ltd, Ringwood, Victoria, Australia
Penguin Books Canada Ltd, 2801 John Street, Markham, Ontario, Canada L3R 1B4
Penguin Books (NZ) Ltd, 182-190 Wairau Road, Auckland 10, New Zealand

Penguin Books Ltd, Registered Offices: Harmondsworth, Middlesex, England

First published 1987
5   7   9   8   6   4

ISBN 0 7232 3457 4

Designed by Bet Ayer

Printed and bound in Great Britain by William Clowes Limited,
Beccles and London

British Library Cataloguing in Publication Data available

CONTENTS

I had long wanted to work on a book of knitting designs which would not be ultra-modern knits for a limited market lasting only a few months, but would be appealing and classic garments to become favourites to be worn for many years.

Both I and my young family were brought up on Peter Rabbit and his friends so perhaps it was not surprising that inspiration came one day when one of my daughters insisted on calling a hare motif on one of my own sweaters Peter Rabbit. Suddenly it all came to life – I was going to do a book based on Beatrix Potter's famous characters! The ideas followed thick and fast and it was sleepless nights for me and my poor husband while I made endless notes as the designs flashed into my mind and took shape. I knew at last what I was going to do and the feeling of excitement was intense – I could not wait to get started!

Within three weeks I had put all my ideas down on paper in sketch form and I hastily worked on a rough book design which I took along to Frederick Warne. The publishers were so enthusiastic that before I knew where I was the book was under way.

I wanted to include something for all the family and also designs for both the inexperienced knitter and those who enjoy more of a challenge. So there are many designs in simple stocking stitch as well as others with more intricate stitch detail, though even these I hope can be tackled by the reasonably experienced knitter.

Although Beatrix Potter's little books are world-famous, it is not so widely known that in later life she became a farmer and was specially interested in the introduction and promotion of Herdwick sheep in her beloved Cumbrian countryside. This hardy breed produces a coarse, long, thick coat which in its untreated form is waterproof and comes in interesting shades of browns and neutrals. Its durability and hard-wearing qualities make it an ideal yarn for tough outdoor wear with an ethnic feel. I therefore decided to include two designs featuring Herdwick wool manufactured by a top British spinner – an appealing and very easy-to-knit children's sweater and cap and also a more elaborate wrap-around, swirly cape – all guaranteed to keep out the cold on autumn days! Both designs have been photographed with Herdwick sheep on one of Beatrix Potter's own farms.

As well as using familiar and well-loved characters such as Benjamin Bunny and Mrs. Tiggy-Winkle as motifs on easy-to-wear children's sweaters, I have also designed several patterns which I feel evoke the beauty of the Lake District. There is a landscape sweater worked in a soft mohair yarn which includes details from Mrs. Tabitha Twitchit's garden, together with flashes of mountain, dry stone walls and lakeland flora all worked in typical delicate Beatrix Potter colouring. Foxgloves appear everywhere in the Peter Rabbit books and so there is a gentle, soft sweater with easy-to-knit foxglove panels. This is pretty enough to wear to a party if you stitch one or two pearl-drop beads to each foxglove bell. There is also a sumptuous christening dress which I hope you will cherish enough to keep as a family heirloom. Peter's famous blue jacket appears too in the form of a smart, blue Aran-style lumber jacket – with, of course, brass buttons! Although it has been made up in blue, this jacket would look wonderful in white or cream as a stunning summer jacket. And men have not been forgotten, with such designs as a sweater featuring Tommy Brock the badger who went to bed with his boots on!

Most of the designs in the book were photographed in and around Sawrey and High Tilberthwaite in the Lake District and I have to thank Frederick Warne and the National Trust for being so cooperative and sensitive to my natural instincts and allowing me to photograph the garments just as I had visualized them in their natural Cumbrian surroundings. The Jeremy Fisher sweater was actually photographed on Esthwaite Water – the setting for his Tale. The Peter Rabbit mother and daughter sweaters and Peter's blue jacket were photographed in Jemima Puddle-Duck's farmyard at Hill Top. If you look at the photograph of the Tom Kitten sweater on page 48 you will see clearly the path and porch at Hill Top. Hill Top was of course Beatrix Potter's first and favourite Lake District home and it was here that she wrote so many of the famous Tales. The photograph of the white party smock was taken inside Hill Top with the fire lit, just as it appears in *The Tale of Samuel Whiskers*; with the fire roaring, suddenly the whole house became alive with the sound of crackling logs and I could capture for a few wonderful moments that very real world of Beatrix Potter – what better inspiration could I have had than her beside me?

I do hope you will enjoy using this book as much as I have enjoyed writing it, producing it and making all the Beatrix Potter characters come to life for you, with the help of Tony Boase, our brilliant photographer, who managed to capture the very essence and sensitivity of Beatrix Potter's world.

PAT MENCHINI

The National Trust in Lakeland

Many of the photographs in this book were taken on National Trust land, at Hill Top, Beatrix Potter's first Lakeland home in the little village of Sawrey, and at High Tilberthwaite, one of the fourteen farms she left to the Trust in her will. High Tilberthwaite is farmed by the son-in-law and daughter of the tenant farmer of Beatrix Potter's own time, and it is still a typical Lakeland hill farm run on traditional lines according to the Trust's policy of preserving the traditional agricultural community which is the life-blood of the whole area. The sheep are Herdwicks, the hardiest of Britain's breeds, whose wiry wool is naturally weatherproof – one fell farmer has worn his Herdwick tweed coat for twenty-eight years in all weathers.

Beatrix Potter worked closely with the National Trust, a charity which now protects over one quarter of the Lake District National Park, for over thirty years, using her book royalties to buy land and buildings, and managing several farms herself on the Trust's behalf. She shared the Trust's concern to conserve the most valuable aspects of the Lake District farmer's traditional way of life and working methods, and to maintain the landscape and buildings for future generations to continue to enjoy.

BEFORE YOU START

- Read through the instructions before you commence and always work in the order stated in the pattern.

- As many of the designs are in a wide size range, it will be found helpful to underline all figures for the size required before commencing. Where only one set of figures is given, this applies to all sizes.

- There are some useful notes on page 124 on designs with colour motifs to help the inexperienced knitter.

- Do read the notes on tension on page 124 before starting a design.

- **Have you checked your tension?**

PETER RABBIT
SWEATER AND ACCESSORIES

Old Mrs. Rabbit was a widow; she earned her living by knitting
rabbit-wool mittens and muffetees (I once bought a pair at a bazaar).

THE TALE OF BENJAMIN BUNNY

SWEATER – MEASUREMENTS

To fit chest	61	66	71	76	81	86	cm
	24	26	28	30	32	34	in
Length from	39	44	48	51	53	56	cm
shoulder	15½	17½	19	20	21	22	in
Sleeve seam,	24	29	37	37	38	38	cm
approx	9½	11½	14½	14½	15	15	in

SWEATER – MATERIALS
Patons Beehive Shetland Chunky, 50 g balls

Pink (M)	4	5	6	7	8	8

1 ball (50 g) each in Brown (A), Blue (B) and White (C).
4 buttons. Oddment of black embroidery thread.
A pair each 6 mm/No 4 and 5 mm/No 2 needles.

ACCESSORIES – MEASUREMENTS

To fit a child aged approx	3–6	7–10	11–14	
SCARF				
length, approx	91	107	117	cm
	36	42	46	in
LEG-WARMERS				
length	20	28	38	cm
	8	11	15	in
HAT				
width round crown,	49	52	54	cm
approx	19½	20½	21½	in
MITTS				
width above thumb,	14	17	19	cm
approx	5½	6½	7½	in
wrist to top of fingers,	13	14	18	cm
approx (adjustable)	5	5¾	7	in

ACCESSORIES – MATERIALS
Patons Beehive Shetland Chunky, 50 g balls

SCARF

White (C)	1	2	2

1 ball (50 g) each in Brown (A), Blue (B) and Pink (M).

LEG-WARMERS

Pink (M)	1	2	2

A small oddment each in Brown (A), Blue (B) and White (C).
Shirring elastic. Oddment of black embroidery thread.

HAT
1 ball (50 g) each in Pink (M) and White (C) for all sizes, and
large oddments in Brown (A) and Blue (B).

MITTS
1 ball (50 g) in Pink (M) for all sizes.
A pair each 7 mm/No 2 for Scarf; a pair each 6 mm/No 4 and
5 mm/No 6 needles for Leg-warmers and Hat; a pair
5 mm/No 6 needles for Mitts.

TENSION
15 sts and 20 rows to 10 cm/4 in over st st on 6 mm/No 4
needles.

ABBREVIATIONS
K = knit; p = purl; sts = stitches; g st = garter st; st st =
stocking st; inc = increase, increasing; dec = decrease,
decreasing; m1 = make 1 by picking up and working into
back of horizontal strand lying before next st; beg =
beginning; alt = alternate; rep = repeat; tog = together; tbl =
through back of loops; cm = centimetres; in = inches; M =
Pink; A = Brown; B = Blue; C = White.

NB: When working from chart twist colours on wrong side
when changing colour.

SWEATER

BACK
With 5 mm needles and A, cast on 44(48, 51, 55, 58, 62) sts.
Work g st border thus: K 1 row A, then 2 rows C, 2 rows M, 2
rows C, 2 rows B. Break A, B and C. Continue in M and k 1
row.**
Next row – P, inc 5(5, 6, 6, 7, 7) sts evenly across.   *49(53, 57, 61, 65, 69) sts.*

Change to 6 mm needles, and, beg with a k row, work 20(24, 26, 28, 30, 32) rows in st st.

***Change to 5 mm needles** and, joining in and breaking off
colours as required, work g st border thus: k 2 rows A, 2 rows
C, 2 rows M, 2 rows C, 2 rows B.**** Break A, B and C.

Change to 6 mm needles and work in st st in M until back
measures 37(42, 46, 48, 51, 53) cm/14½(16½, 18, 19, 20, 21) in
from beg, ending after a p row.
Work from *** to **** again, omitting final row in B. Cast off
loosely in B.

POCKET LININGS (2)
With 6 mm needles and M, cast on 14(15, 16, 18, 19, 20) sts. Work 20(22, 24, 26, 28, 30) rows in st st. Slip sts on a spare needle.

FRONT
Work as back to **** but omit final row in B.

Place pocket linings thus:
Next row – In B, k4(5, 6, 6, 7, 8), *cast off next 14(15, 16, 18, 19, 20) sts loosely knitways*, k13 (including st on needle after cast-off), work from * to *, k to end.
Break A, B and C and **change to 6 mm needles.** Continue in M.
Next row – K4(5, 6, 6, 7, 8), k across a group of lining sts, k13, k across a group of lining sts, k to end.
Continue in st st until front measures 6(6, 8, 8, 8, 10) rows less than back up to striped shoulder border, ending after a p row.

Shape neck thus:
Next row – K20(21, 23, 24, 26, 27), turn.
Continue on this group. Dec 1 st at neck edge on next 3 rows. *17(18, 20, 21, 23, 24) sts.*
Work 2(2, 4, 4, 4, 6) rows straight. Work from *** to **** as on back, but omit final row in B. Cast off *loosely* in B.

With right side facing, slip centre 9(11, 11, 13, 13, 15) sts on a spare needle. Rejoin M. K 1 row. Complete as first side.

SLEEVES
Commencing with 34(35, 37, 38, 41, 42) sts, work as back to **.
Next row – P, inc 5(6, 6, 7, 8, 9) sts evenly across. *39(41, 43, 45, 49, 51) sts.*

Change to 6 mm needles, and, beg with a k row, work 10(18, 32, 32, 32, 32) rows in st st.
Continue in st st, **working from Chart 1** thus:

CHART 1

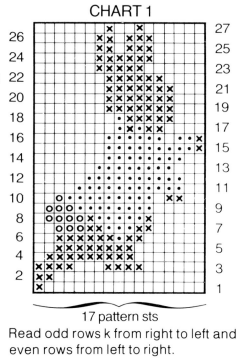

KEY

□ = M (Pink)

✕ = A (Brown)

• = B (Blue)

o = C (White)

Use a separate small ball of A, B and C for each colour area, and a separate ball of M at each side of Peter's body on rows 3 to 24.

17 pattern sts

Read odd rows k from right to left and even rows from left to right.

1st row – 11(12, 13, 14, 16, 17)M, work 1st row of chart, 11(12, 13, 14, 16, 17)M.
2nd to 27th rows – Rep 1st row 26 times, but working rows 2 to 27 of Chart 1.
Continue in M only for a few rows until sleeve measures 24(29, 37, 37, 38, 38) cm/9½(11½, 14½, 14½, 15, 15) in from beg. Cast off *loosely*.

FRONT NECK BORDER
With 5 mm needles and A, right side facing, k up 31(33, 37, 39, 39, 43) sts evenly round front neck, including shoulder borders and sts on spare needle. Work in g st thus: K 1 row A, 2 rows C, 2 rows M, 2 rows C, 1 row B. Cast off in B, working firmly in front corners.

TO MAKE UP
First embroider nose, whiskers, eye and shoes in black embroidery cotton on Peter. Then highlight edge of collar and sleeve. Add white to eye using a split length of C.** Sew down pocket linings on wrong side. Join shoulders, leaving approx 6 cm/2½ in free at each neck edge. Stitch cast-off edges of sleeves to yoke, then join side and sleeve seams. Work 4 loops in buttonhole stitch on front shoulders and neck border, then sew buttons to correspond on back edge.

SCARF

With 7 mm needles and A, cast on 116(136, 148) sts loosely. K 1 row.
Work in g st in stripes of 2 rows C, 2 rows M, 2 rows C, 2 rows B, 2 rows C, 2 rows A, repeated throughout until scarf measures approx 14(17, 19) cm/5½(6½, 7½) in, ending after 2 rows C, 1 row A. Cast off loosely in A.

Make 2 pompons in C (or colours as desired). Run an end along each short end of scarf, draw up tightly and fasten off. Attach a pompon to each end.

LEG-WARMERS

Begin at ankle. **With 5 mm needles and M,** cast on 29(33, 39) sts loosely.
1st row (right side) – K2, [p1, k1] to last st, k1.
2nd row – K1, [p1, k1] to end.
Work 2(4, 4) more rows in rib.

Change to 6 mm needles and, beg with a k row, work 2(14, 30) rows in st st with p rows having k1 at each end, while inc 1 st at each end of 11th row on 2nd size only and inc 1 st at each end of 21st and 27th rows on 3rd size only. *29(35, 43) sts.*

Continue in st st, **working from Chart 1** thus:
1st row – 6(9, 13)M, work 1st row of chart, 6(9, 13)M.
Continue with chart as placed on last row, working rows 2 to 27, at the same time shape leg by inc 1 st at each end of 2nd row following, then on every following 6th row, until there are 37(43, 51) sts, taking extra sts into M.
Work 3(5, 7) rows straight in M, dec 2(4, 4) sts evenly on last row. *35(39, 47) sts.*

Change to **5 mm needles** and work 6 rows in rib as at commencement. Cast off loosely in rib.
Make a second leg-warmer the same.

TO MAKE UP
Make up as Sweater to **. Join seam. Run 2–3 rows of shirring elastic through wrong side of top band of rib, drawing up slightly.

HAT

EAR-FLAPS
With 5 mm needles and C, cast on 6(8, 9) sts and k 1 row.
Next row – In M, inc in first st, k to last st, inc in last st.
Next row – In M, k.
Rep the last 2 rows twice, working 2 rows in C, 2 rows in B. *12(14, 15) sts.*
Continue in g st, working 2 rows C, 2 rows A, 2 rows C, 2 rows M.
Slip sts on a spare needle. Make another ear-flap the same but leave sts on needle.

With C, cast on 13 sts on to empty 5 mm needle and, using this needle and C, k across group of ear-flap sts, cast on 23(23, 25) sts, k across 2nd group of ear-flap sts, finally cast on 13 sts. *73(77, 81) sts.*
Keeping continuity of stripes correct, work 7 rows in g st. Break A, B and C.
Continue in M.

Change to 6 mm needles and st st, p rows having k1 at each end, until work measures 9(10; 10) cm/3½(4, 4) in from 23(23, 25) cast-on sts, ending after a p row and dec 4 sts evenly on last row on 2nd size only. *73(73, 81) sts.*

3rd size only
Next row – [K8, k2 tog] 8 times, k1.
Next row – k1, p71, k1.

All sizes
Shape crown thus:
1st row – [K7, k2 tog] 8 times, k1.
2nd and alt rows – k1, p to last st, k1.
3rd row – [K6, k2 tog] 8 times, k1.
5th row – [K5, k2 tog] 8 times, k1.
Continue thus, dec 8 sts on every k row, until 17 sts remain. Work 1 row. Break yarn. Thread end through sts, draw up and fasten off.

BORDER
With 5 mm needles and A, right side facing, k up 13 sts from first section of cast-on sts of back of hat, 22(24, 25) sts *evenly* round right ear-flap, 23(23, 25) sts from centre, 22(24, 25) sts *evenly* round left ear-flap, finally 13 sts from second section of back. *93(97, 101) sts.*
K 1 row A, 2 rows C, 1 row M. Cast off evenly knitways in M, working *loosely* round ear-flaps.

TO MAKE UP
Join seam. With C make a pompon and attach to top of crown.

MITTS

RIGHT MITT
With 5 mm needles and M, cast on 23(25; 29) sts. Work 10(12, 14) rows in rib as on Leg-warmers.
Change to st st and, beg with a k row, work 2 rows, p row having k1 at each end.**

Shape thumb gusset thus:
1st row – K13(14, 16), m1, k1, m1, k9(10, 12).
2nd and alt rows – K1, p to last st, k1.
3rd row – K13(14, 16), m1, k3, m1, k to end.
5th row – K13(14, 16), m1, k5, m1, k to end. ***Continue in this way, inc 2 sts every k row, until 1(2, 3) more sets of increases have been worked. *31(35, 41) sts.*
Next row – K1, p to last st, k1.***

Work thumb thus:
Next row – K22(25, 29), turn.
****Next row** – Cast on 1 st, p8(10, 12), k1, turn.
Work 8(10, 12) rows in st st on these 10(12, 14) sts.
Next row – k2 tog 5(6, 7) times.
Work 1 row. Break yarn, thread through sts, draw up and fasten off securely.

With right side facing, rejoin M to base of thumb and k up 1 st from cast-on st, k to end. *23(25, 29) sts.*
Work 15(17, 21) rows in st st. (Length may be adjusted here.)

Shape top thus:
1st row – K1, *k2 tog tbl, k6(7; 9), k2 tog, k1; rep from * once.
2nd row – K1, p to last st, k1.
3rd row – K1, *k2 tog tb1, k4(5, 7) k2 tog, k1; rep from * once.

3rd size only
4th row – K1, p to last st, k1.
5th row – K1, *k2 tog tbl, k5, k2 tog, k1; rep from * once.

All sizes
Work 1 row. Cast off.

LEFT MITT
Work as right mitt to **.

Shape thumb gusset thus:
1st row – K9(10, 12), m1, k1, m1, k13(14, 16).
2nd and alt rows – K1, p to last st, k1.
3rd row – K9(10, 12), m1, k3, m1, k to end.
5th row – K9(10, 12), m1, k5, m1, k to end.
Work as right mitt from *** to ***.

Work thumb thus:
Next row – K18(21, 25), turn.
Complete as right mitt, working from **** to end.

TO MAKE UP
Join seams.

11

MRS. TIGGY-WINKLE
SWEATER

Mrs. Tiggy-winkle's nose went sniffle, sniffle, snuffle, and her eyes went twinkle, twinkle; and she fetched another hot iron from the fire.
THE TALE OF MRS. TIGGY-WINKLE

MEASUREMENTS

To fit chest	56	61	66	71	cm
	22	24	26	28	in
Length at centre back	41	44	48	52	cm
excluding neckband,	16	17½	19	20½	in
approx					
Sleeve seam	25	29	33	37	cm
	10	11½	13	14½	in

MATERIALS
Lister Motoravia D K, 50 g balls

Cream (M)	5	6	6	7

1 ball (50 g) in Pink (A); an oddment each in Dark Grey, White, Seagreen, Emerald, Camel, Light Grey, Mid-Brown and Dark Brown. A pair each 4 mm / No 8 and 3¼ mm / No 10 needles. Set of four 3¼ mm / No 10 needles. 1 black sequin or small button for eye.

TENSION
22 sts and 30 rows to 10 cm/4 in over st st on 4 mm/No 8 needles.

ABBREVIATIONS
K = knit; kb = k into back of next st; p = purl; sts = stitches; st st = stocking st; inc = increase, increasing; dec = decrease, decreasing; beg = beginning; rep = repeat; tog = together; foll = following; tbl = through back of loops; cm = centimetres; in = inches; M = main colour (cream); A = 1st contrast (pink).

FRONT
With 3¼ mm needles and A, cast on 61(67, 73, 79) sts.
**1st row (right side) – K1, [kb, p1] to last 2 sts, kb, k1.
2nd row – K1, [p1, k1] to end. Break A.
Join in M and rib 17(21, 21, 25) more rows.******
Next row – Rib 6(3, 6, 3), *inc in next st, rib 3(4, 4, 5); rep from * to last 7(4, 7, 4) sts, inc in next st, rib to end.   *74(80, 86, 92) sts.*
Change to 4 mm needles and, beg with a k row, work 20(24, 32, 36) rows in st st.

Using small balls of yarn for each colour area where possible, otherwise carrying colour not in use loosely over not more than 5 sts at a time twisting yarns on wrong side when changing colour, continue in st st, **working from Chart 2** (see page 14) thus:
1st row – 19(22, 25, 28)M, work 1st row of chart, 19(22, 25, 28)M.
2nd to 32nd rows – Rep 1st row 31 times, but working rows 2 to 32 of Chart 2.

Keeping chart correct and noting that when 48th row of chart has been worked all sts should be worked in M, **shape raglan** thus:
1st and 2nd rows – Cast off 2 sts, work to end.
3rd row – K2, k2 tog tbl, k to last 4 sts, k2 tog, k2.
4th row – K1, p1, p2 tog, p to last 4 sts, p2 tog tbl, p1, k1.
5th row – As 3rd.
6th row – K1, p to last st, k1.*******
Rep 5th and 6th rows only until 34(38, 42, 46) sts remain, ending after a 6th row.

Shape neck thus:
Next row – k2, k2 tog tbl, k7(8, 9, 10), turn.
Continue on this group. Still dec at raglan edge as before, *at the same time* dec 1 st at neck edge on next 3 rows.   *6(7, 8, 9) sts.*
Continue dec at raglan edge only until 2 sts remain. Work 1 row. Fasten off.

With right side facing, slip centre 12(14, 16, 18) sts on a spare needle. Rejoin M and k to last 4 sts, k2 tog, k2. Complete as first side.

BACK
Omitting motif, work as front to *******. Rep 5th and 6th rows only until 22(24, 26, 28) sts remain, ending after a 6th row. Slip sts on a spare needle.

SLEEVES
With 3¼ mm needles and A, cast on 33(35, 37, 39) sts. Work as front from ****** to ******.
Next row – Rib 2(3, 4, 5), [inc in next st, rib 2] 9 times, inc in next st, rib to end.   *43(45, 47, 49) sts.*

Change to 4 mm needles and, beg with a k row, work in st st, shaping sleeve by inc 1 st at each end of 5th row and then on every foll 6th row until there are 59(63, 67, 71) sts. Work

CHART 2

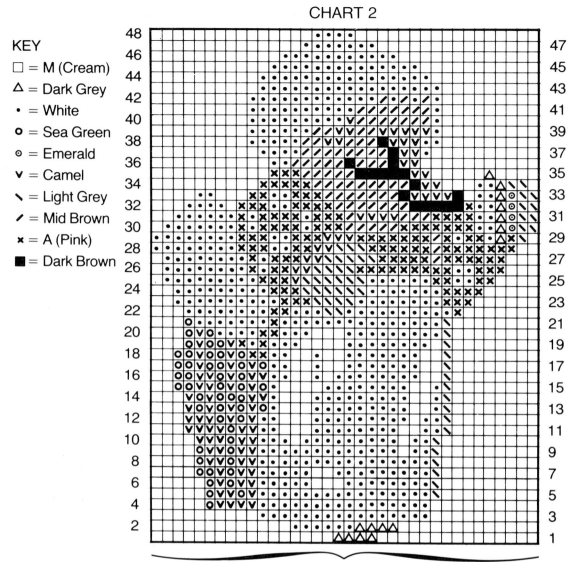

KEY

☐ = M (Cream)
△ = Dark Grey
• = White
○ = Sea Green
◉ = Emerald
v = Camel
⟍ = Light Grey
⟋ = Mid Brown
✕ = A (Pink)
■ = Dark Brown

36 pattern sts

Read odd rows k from right to left and even rows p from left to right.

straight until sleeve measures 25(29, 33, 37) cm / 10(11½, 13, 14½) in from beg, ending after a p row.

Shape raglan thus:
1st to 6th rows – As on front.
Rep 5th and 6th rows only until 7 sts remain, ending after a 6th row. Slip sts on a spare needle.

NECKBAND

First join raglan shapings. **With set of 3¼ mm needles and M**, right side facing, k across back sts inc 9 sts evenly, k across sts of left sleeve inc 3 sts on 2 smallest sizes, k up 11(13, 15, 17) sts down left front neck, k across centre sts inc 3 sts evenly, k up 11(13, 15, 17) sts up right front neck, finally k across sts of right sleeve inc 3 sts on 2 smallest sizes. *88(96, 98, 106) sts.*
1st round – [Kb, p1] to end.
2nd round – [K1, p1] to end.
Rep the last 2 rounds 7(8, 8, 9) times more. Cast off *loosely*.

TO MAKE UP

Using dark brown (split if necessary), embroider prickles and nose. Using dark grey, embroider claws, then outline in backstitch the back of dress, petticoat, sleeve, lower edge of apron and iron. Using pink, embroider flowers on dress. Sew sequin/button in position for eye. Omitting ribbing, press, following pressing instructions on ball band. Join side and sleeve seams. Fold neckband in half to wrong side and hem in position. Press seams.

14

APPLEY DAPPLY
HOODED JACKET

Appley Dapply has little sharp eyes,
And Appley Dapply is so fond of pies!
APPLEY DAPPLY'S NURSERY RHYMES

MEASUREMENTS

To fit chest	66	71	76	81	86	cm
	26	28	30	32	34	in
Length from	41	47	52	57	58	cm
shoulder	16	18½	20½	22½	23	in
Sleeve seam,	29	34	37	38	40	cm
adjustable	11¾	13¾	14¾	15¼	15¾	in

MATERIALS

Robin Intrigue (M),

50 g balls	7	7	8	8	9

Robin Landscape D K, 1 ball (50 g) each Light (L) and Dark (D).
A pair each 5½ mm / No 5 and 4 mm / No 8 needles. A 35(40, 45, 50, 50) cm or 14(16, 18, 20, 20) in open-ended zip-fastener.

TENSION

16 sts and 20 rows to 10 cm / 4 in over rev st st using 5½ mm / No 5 needles and M.

ABBREVIATIONS

K = knit; p = purl; sts = stitches; (rev)st st = (reverse) stocking st; inc = increase, increasing; dec = decrease, decreasing; foll = following; beg = beginning; tog = together; alt = alternate; rep = repeat; 0 = no sts worked on this particular size; cm = centimetres; in = inches; M = main colour; L = light; D = dark.

BACK

With 4 mm needles and M, cast on 43(47, 51, 55, 59) sts.
1st row (right side) – K2, [p1, k1] to last st, k1.
2nd row – K1, [p1, k1] to end.
Rep these 2 rows for 5(6, 6, 7, 7) cm / 2(2½, 2½, 3, 3) in, ending after a 1st row.
Next row – Rib 1(3, 5, 7, 9), [inc in next st, rib 1] 20 times, inc in next st, rib to end. *64(68, 72, 76, 80) sts.*

Change to 5½ mm needles and, beg with a p row for right side, work 31(37, 45, 49, 49) rows in rev st st.
Next row (wrong side) – P3(3, 2, 2, 2), [inc in next st, p2] 3(3, 4, 4, 4) times, [inc in next st, p1] 21(23, 23, 25, 27) times, [inc in next st, p2] 2(2, 3, 3, 3) times, inc in next st, p to end. *91(97, 103, 109, 115) sts.*

Break M. Join in L. **Change to 4 mm needles** and, beg with a k row, work 2 rows in st st.
Continue in st st with **Dancing Mice from Chart 3** (see page 16) thus:
1st row – 24(27, 30, 33, 36)L, work 1st row of chart, 24(27, 30, 33, 36)L.
2nd to 24th rows – Rep 1st row 23 times, but working rows 2 to 24 of Chart 3. Break D.
K 1 row L.
Next row – In L, p3(3, 2, 2, 2), [p2 tog, p2] 3(3, 4, 4, 4) times, [p2 tog, p1] 21(23, 23, 25, 27) times, [p2 tog, p2] 2(2, 3, 3, 3) times, p2 tog, p to end. *64(68, 72, 76, 80) sts.*

Break L. Join in M. **Change to 5½ mm needles**. K 1 row. Beg with a k row again for wrong side, work in rev st st until back measures 41(47, 52, 57, 58) cm / 16(18½, 20½, 22½, 23) in at centre, ending after a k row.

Shape shoulders thus:
Cast off 8(8, 9, 9, 10) sts at beg of next 4 rows, then 7(8, 8, 9, 9) sts at beg of next 2 rows.

Work back of hood thus:
Continue in rev st st on 18(20, 20, 22, 22) sts, inc 1 st at each end of 7th row foll, then on every foll 8th row until there are 26(28, 28, 30, 30) sts. Work 5(5, 7, 7, 9) rows straight.
Now dec 1 st at each end of next row, then on foll alt row. Work 1 row. Dec 1 st at each end of next 2 rows. *18(20, 20, 22, 22) sts.*

Work front of hood thus:
Continue in rev st st, casting on 10 sts at beg of next 6 rows, then 8(8, 9, 9, 10) sts at beg of foll 2 rows. *94(96, 98, 100, 102) sts.*
Work 16(18, 18, 20, 20) rows straight, inc 5(5, 7, 5, 5) sts evenly on last row. *99(101, 105, 105, 107) sts.*

Change to 4 mm needles and work 8 rows in rib as on back.
Next row (on which holes for cord are worked) – K2(3, 1, 1, 2), [yarn forward, k2 tog, k2] 24(24, 26, 26, 26) times, k1 (2, 0, 0, 1).
Beg with a 2nd row, rib 3 more rows. Cast off loosely in rib.

RIGHT FRONT
With 4 mm needles and M, cast on 21(23, 25, 27, 29) sts.

Work in rib as on back for 5(6, 6, 7, 7) cm/2(2½, 2½, 3, 3) in, ending after a 2nd row and inc 11 sts evenly on last row. *32(34, 36, 38, 40) sts.*

Change to 5½ mm needles and, beg with a p row, work 4(6, 8, 10, 10) rows in rev st st.**

Work pocket thus:
Next row – P21(22, 23, 24, 25), k3, slip remaining 8(9, 10, 11, 12) sts on a spare needle, cast on 3 sts for pocket facing. Continue on 27(28, 29, 30, 31) sts. Working 6 sts at pocket edge in garter st and remainder in rev st st work 20(22, 24, 26, 26) rows, casting off 3 pocket facing sts at end of last row. Slip sts on a length of yarn.

With 5½ mm needles and M, cast on 18(19, 21, 23, 24) sts for lining. Using needle holding these sts, p across sts on spare needle. Work 20(22, 24, 26, 26) rows in rev st st, casting off 18(19, 21, 23, 24) lining sts at beg of last row.
***Next row** – K to end, k across sts on length of yarn. Work 5(7, 11, 11, 11) rows in rev st st.
Next row – [Inc in next 2 sts, p1] twice, [inc in next st, p1] 10(11, 12, 13, 14) times, [inc in next 2 sts, p1] twice. *50(53, 56, 59, 62) sts.*

Break M. Join in L. **Change to 4 mm needles** and, beg with a k row, work 2 rows in st st. **Continue in st st with Dancing Mice from Chart 3** thus:
1st row – 3(4, 5, 6, 7)L, work 1st row of chart, 4(6, 8, 10, 12)L.
2nd row – 4(6, 8, 10, 12)L, work 2nd row of chart, 3(4, 5, 6, 7)L.

3rd to 24th rows – Rep 1st and 2nd rows 11 times but working rows 3 to 24 of Chart 3.
K 1 row L.
Next row – In L, [p2 tog, p1, p2 tog] twice, [p1, p2 tog] 10(11, 12, 13, 14) times, [p2 tog, p1, p2 tog] twice. *32(34, 36, 38, 40) sts.*

Break L. Join in M. **Change to 5½ mm needles** and k 1 row. Beg with a k row, again work in rev st st until front measures 10(12, 12, 12, 14) rows *less* than back up to shoulder shaping, ending at front edge. (NB. Work 1 row less here on left front.)

Shape neck thus:
Cast off 6(7, 7, 8, 8) sts at beg of next row. Dec 1 st at neck edge on next 3 rows. *23(24, 26, 27, 29) sts.*
Work straight until front measures same as back to shoulder shaping, ending at side edge.

Shape shoulder thus:
Cast off 8(8, 9, 9, 10) sts at beg of next and foll alt row. Work 1 row. Cast off.

LEFT FRONT
Work as right front to **

Work pocket thus:
Next row – P8(9, 10, 11, 12), slip remaining 24(25, 26, 27, 28) sts on a spare needle, cast on 18(19, 21, 23, 24) sts for lining. Work 20(22, 24, 26, 26) rows in rev st st, casting off 18(19, 21, 23, 24) lining sts at end of last row. Slip sts on a length of yarn.

CHART 3

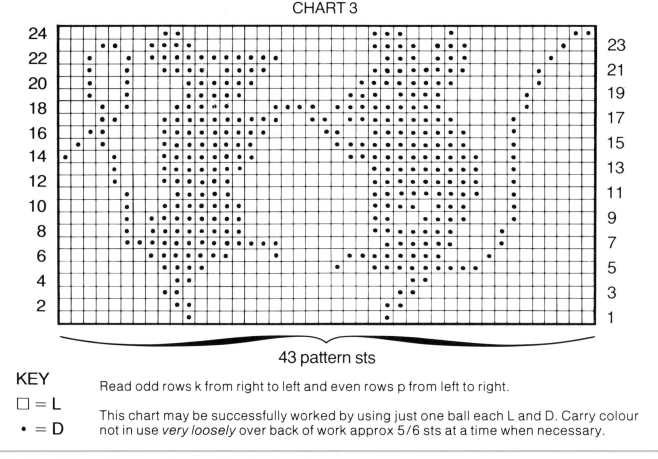

43 pattern sts

KEY

□ = L
• = D

Read odd rows k from right to left and even rows p from left to right.

This chart may be successfully worked by using just one ball each L and D. Carry colour not in use *very loosely* over back of work approx 5/6 sts at a time when necessary.

With 5½ mm needles and M, cast on 3 sts, using needle holding these sts, k3, p to end across sts on spare needle. Working 6 sts at pocket edge in garter st and remainder in rev st st, work 20(22, 24, 26, 26) rows, casting off 3 pocket facing sts at beg of last row.

Complete to match right front, working from *** to end, noting that 1st row placing chart will commence: 4(6, 8, 10, 12)L.

SLEEVES

With 4 mm needles and M, cast on 27(29, 29, 31, 31) sts. Work 5(6, 6, 7, 7) cm/2(2½, 2½, 3, 3) in in rib as on back, ending after a 2nd row.

Next row – P, inc once in every st.

Next row – K, inc 1(1, 4, 2, 5) sts evenly.   55(59, 62, 64, 67) sts.

Change to 5½ mm needles and, beg with a p row, continue in rev st st until sleeve measures 29(34, 37, 38, 40) cm/11¾(13¾, 14¾, 15¼, 15¾) in from beg. Cast off loosely. (N B. Length may be adjusted here.)

TO MAKE UP

Do not press. Fold 3 pocket facing sts to wrong side and hem in position. Sew down pocket linings lightly on wrong side. Stitch shaped cast-on edges of front of hood to side edges of back of hood. Fold ribbing of front of hood in half to wrong side and hem in position. Stitch side edge of hood in position to front neck. Stitch cast-off edge of sleeves in position to yoke. Join side and sleeve seams. Sew in zip. Using 2 lengths each L and D, make a twisted cord and slot through holes round inside edge of front of hood, knotting and trimming ends to form tassels. (For how to make cords, see making up of oblong cushion, pages 110–11.)

MR. JEREMY FISHER
SWEATER

Mr. Jeremy stuck his pole into the mud and fastened his boat to it. Then he settled himself cross-legged and arranged his fishing tackle.

THE TALE OF MR. JEREMY FISHER

MEASUREMENTS

To fit chest	61	66	71	cm
	24	26	28	in
Length at centre back,	44	48	52	cm
excluding neckband, approx	17½	19	20½	in
Sleeve seam	29	33	37	cm
	11½	13	14½	in

MATERIALS

Lister Bamboo Quartz (M),
50 g balls 6 6 7
Large oddments of any Lister Double Knitting each in Dark Green, Red, Oyster and Camel and small oddments in Light Green, White, Black and Yellow.
A pair each 4 mm/No 8 and 3 mm/No 11 needles. Set of four 3 mm/No 11 needles. Small quantity of washable filling.

TENSION

22 sts and 30 rows to 10 cm/4in over st st on 4 mm/No 8 needles.

ABBREVIATIONS

K = knit; kb = k into back of next st; p = purl; sts = stitches; st st = stocking st; inc = increase, increasing; dec = decrease, decreasing; beg = beginning; rep = repeat; tog = together; foll = following; sl = slip; tbl = through back of loops; M = main shade; cm = centimetres; in = inches.

FRONT

With 3 mm needles and M, cast on 67(73, 79) sts.
**1st row (right side) – K1, [kb, p1] to last 2 sts, kb, k1.
2nd row – K1, [p1, k1] to end.
Work 17(21, 25) more rows in rib.**
Next row – Rib 3(6, 3), *inc in next st, rib 4(4, 5); rep from * to last 4(7, 4) sts, inc in next st, rib to end.   *80(86, 92) sts.*

Change to 4 mm needles and, beg with a k row, work 10(14, 18) rows in st st.

Using separate balls of yarn for each colour area, and twisting yarns on wrong side when changing colour, continue in st st, **working from Chart 4** (see page 20) thus:

1st row – 7(10, 13)M, work 1st row of chart, 12(15,18)M.
2nd row – 12(15, 18)M, work 2nd row of chart, 7(10, 13)M.
3rd to 50th rows – Rep 1st and 2nd rows 24 times but working rows 3 to 50 of Chart 4.

Keeping chart correct and noting that when 70th row of chart has been worked all sts should be worked in M, **shape raglan** thus:
1st and 2nd rows – Cast off 2 sts, work to end.
3rd row – K1, k2 tog tbl, k to last 3 sts, k2 tog, k1.
4th row – K1, p2 tog, p to last 3 sts, p2 tog tbl, k1.
5th row – As 3rd.
6th row – K1, p to last st, k1.*****
Rep 5th and 6th rows only until 38(42, 46) sts remain, ending after a 6th row.

Shape neck thus:
Next row – K1, k2 tog tbl, k9(10, 11), turn.
Continue on this group. Still dec at raglan edge as before, at the same time dec 1 st at neck edge on next 3 rows.   *7(8, 9) sts.*
Continue dec at raglan edge only until 2 sts remain. Work 1 row. Fasten off.

With right side facing, slip centre 14(16, 18) sts on a spare needle. Rejoin M and k to last 3 sts, k2 tog, k1. Complete as first side.

BACK

Omitting motif, work as front to *****. Rep 5th and 6th rows only until 24(26, 28) sts remain, ending after a 6th row. Slip sts on a spare needle.

SLEEVES

With 3 mm needles and M, cast on 35(37, 39) sts. Work as front from ** to **.
Next row – Rib 3(4, 5), [inc in next st, rib 2] 9 times, inc in next st, rib to end.   *45(47, 49) sts.*

Change to 4 mm needles and, beg with a k row, work in st st, shaping sleeve by inc 1 st at each end of 5th row, then on every foll 6th row until there are 63(67, 71) sts. Work straight until sleeve measures 29(33, 37) cm/11½(13, 14½) in from beg, ending after a p row.

CHART 4

61 pattern sts

KEY □ = M   ✕ = Oyster   ╱ = White

− = Dark Green   ∧ = Camel

• = Red   ╲ = Light Green

Read odd rows k from right to left
and even rows p from left to right.

Shape raglan thus:
1st to 6th rows – As on front.
Rep 5th and 6th rows only until 7 sts remain, ending after a 6th row. Slip sts on a spare needle.

NECKBAND

First join raglan shapings. **With set of 3 mm needles and M**, right side facing, k across back sts inc 7 sts evenly, k across sts of left sleeve, k up 13(15, 17) sts down left front neck, k across centre sts inc 3 sts evenly, k up 13(15, 17) sts up right front neck, finally k across sts of right sleeve.   *88(96, 104) sts.*
1st round – [Kb, p1] to end.
2nd round – [K1, p1] to end.
Rep these 2 rounds 6(7, 8) times more. Cast off *loosely*.

HEAD

With 3 mm needles and Camel, cast on 22 sts. P 1 row.
Shape thus:
1st row – [K4, m1 by picking up and knitting into back of horizontal strand lying before next st] twice, k6, [m1, k4] twice.   *26 sts.*
2nd, 4th and 6th rows – P.
3rd row – [K5, m1] twice, k6, [m1, k5] twice.   *30 sts.*
5th row – [K6, m1] twice, k6, [m1, k6] twice.   *34 sts.*
7th row – K to last 4 sts, turn.
8th row – Sl 1, p to last 4 sts, turn. Continue in st st.
9th and 10th rows – Sl 1, work to last 8 sts, turn.
11th and 12th rows – Sl 1, work to last 12 sts, turn.
13th row – Sl 1, k to end.
14th row (on which ridge for mouth is worked) – P5, k24, p5.
15th to 18th rows – Beg with a k row, work 4 rows in st st.
19th row – K11, [sl 1, k2 tog, pass slipped st over, k6] twice, k5.   *30 sts.*

20th row – P2 tog, p to last 2 sts, p2 tog.   *28 sts.*
21st row – K2 tog, k6, [sl 1, k2 tog, pass slipped st over, k6] twice, k2 tog.   *22 sts.*
22nd row – As 20th.   *20 sts.*
23rd row – K2 tog, k2, [m1, k1] 4 times, m1, k4, [m1, k1] 4 times, m1, k2, k2 tog.   *28 sts.*
24th row – P2 tog, p10, cast off 4 centre sts, p to last 2 sts, p2 tog. Continue on last group of 11 sts.
**25th row – K to last st, turn.
26th row – Sl 1, p to last st, turn.
27th and 28th rows – Sl 1, work to last 2 sts, turn.
29th and 30th rows – Sl 1, work to last 3 sts, turn.
31st row – Sl 1, k to end.
32nd row – P3 tog, [p2 tog] 4 times. Cast off.**

With right side facing, rejoin yarn to remaining 11 sts and work from ** to **.

LEGS (2 alike)

Begin at toes. **With 3 mm needles and Black**, cast on 6 sts and k 1 row.
Next row – P, inc once in every st.   *12 sts.*
Continue in st st and work 4 rows in Black, 2 rows in White, [2 rows Yellow, 4 rows Camel] 10 times. Cast off in Camel.

TO MAKE UP

Press work following pressing instructions on ball band, omitting ribbing, motif, head and legs. Embroider eyes in black on Mr. Jeremy's head, then sew head in position to body, stuffing as you go. Join toes and join side edges of legs; sew legs in position as in photograph. Join side and sleeve seams. Fold neckband in half to wrong side and hem in position. Press seams. If desired, catch Mr. Jeremy's legs together crosslegged.

HERDWICK
CHILD'S SWEATER, OVERTOP AND CAP

'What are these dear soft fluffy things?' said Lucie.
'Oh those are woolly coats belonging to the little lambs at Skelghyl.'
'Will their jackets take off?' asked Lucie.
'Oh yes, if you please'm; look at the sheep-mark on the shoulder. And
here's one marked for Gatesgarth, and three that come from Littletown.
They're always marked at washing!' said Mrs. Tiggy-winkle.

THE TALE OF MRS. TIGGY-WINKLE

MEASUREMENTS

To fit chest	56–61	61–66	66–71	cm
	22–24	*24–26*	*26–28*	*in*
Length from shoulder	41	44	48	cm
	16	*17½*	*19*	*in*
Sleeve seam (Sweater),	23	29	36	cm
approx	*9¼*	*11½*	*14*	*in*

MATERIALS
SWEATER

Lister Herdwick (M),			
50 g balls	4	5	6
Lister Pure Wool Aran (C),			
50 g balls	3	3	3
OVERTOP			
Lister Herdwick (M),			
50 g balls	4	4	5
Lister Pure Wool Aran (C),			
50 g balls	1	1	2

CAP
Lister Herdwick or **Lister Pure Wool Aran**, 2 balls (50 g)
A pair each 5 mm/No 6 and 4 mm/No 8 needles. Length of
petersham ribbon and 1 button for Cap.

TENSION
18 sts and 22 rows to 10 cm/4 in over st st on 5 mm/No 6
needles.

ABBREVIATIONS
K = knit; p = purl; sts = stitches; st st = stocking st; g st =
garter st; inc = increase, increasing; patt = pattern; tog =
together; sl = slip; beg = beginning; rep = repeat; cm =
centimetres; in = inches; M = Herdwick; C = Pure Wool
Aran.

SWEATER

FRONT AND BACK (2 pieces alike)
Begin at top edge. **With 5 mm needles and C**, cast on
126(146, 166) sts. **Work 7 rows in g st.

Change to ridge patt thus:
1st to 4th rows – In M, beg with a k row work 4 rows in st st.
5th to 8th rows – In C, work 4 rows in g st.
Rep 1st to 8th rows twice more. Break off C.**
Continue in M and, beg with a k row, continue straight in st
st until work measures 13(14, 16) cm/5(5¾, 6¼) in at centre.

Shape sleeve thus:
Cast off 5 sts at beg of next 2 rows, then 7(9, 11) sts at beg of
next 8 rows. *60(64, 68) sts.*
Continue straight until work measures 34(37, 39) cm/
13½(14½, 15½) in from beg, measured through centre of
work, ending after a p row and decreasing 8 st evenly on last
row. *52(56, 60) sts.*

***Change to 4 mm needles and rib** thus:
1st row – K3, [p2, k2] to last st, k1.
2nd row – K1, [p2, k2] to last 3 sts, p2, k1.
Rep these 2 rows for 6(7, 9) cm/2½(3, 3½) in, ending after a
1st row. Cast off *loosely* in rib.***

GUSSETS (2 alike)
With 4 mm needles and C, cast on 12 sts. Work 3 rows in g st.
Continue in g st, decreasing 1 st at each end of next row and
every following 4th row until 2 sts remain. Work 1 row.
Fasten off.

CUFFS
Leaving approx centre 48(50, 52) sts free for neck and gussets, join remainder of cast-on edges of back and front to
form shoulder seams. Sew gussets neatly in position to
shoulders, noting that cast-on edges will form neck edge and
leaving approx 22(24, 26) sts free on back and front for
neck.**

With **4 mm needles and C**, right side facing, k up 28(28, 32) sts evenly and firmly along lower edge of sleeve. Beg with a 2nd row, work in rib as on welt for 5(6, 7) cm/2(2½, 3) in, ending after a 1st row. Cast off *loosely* in rib.

TO MAKE UP
Omitting ribbing, press, following pressing instructions on ball band, pressing g st ridges only very lightly. Join side and sleeve seams, including cuffs. Press seams.

OVERTOP

FRONT AND BACK (2 pieces alike)
Begin at top edge. **With 5 mm needles and C**, cast on 62(66, 70) sts. Work as front and back of Sweater from ** to **.
Continue in M and, beg with a k row, work straight in st st until work measures 34(37, 39) cm/13½(14½, 15½) in from beg, measured through centre of work, ending after a p row and decreasing 10 sts evenly on last row.   *52(56, 60) sts.*

Work as front and back of Sweater from *** to ***.

GUSSETS (2 alike)
Work as Sweater.

ARMHOLE BORDERS
Work as cuffs to **.
Place a marker 14(15, 17) cm/5½(6, 6½) in down from shoulder seams on back and front at side edges. **With 4 mm needles and C**, right side facing, k up 48(53, 58) sts evenly between 1 set of markers. Work 6 rows in g st. Cast off evenly knitways.

TO MAKE UP
Press as for Sweater. Join side seams, including armhole borders. Press seams.

CAP

MAIN PART
With 4 mm needles, cast on 92 sts. Knit 3 rows, inc 10 sts evenly on last row.   *102 sts.*
Shape thus:
1st row – [K9, inc in next st] 10 times, k2.
2nd and alternate rows – P.
3rd row – [K10, inc in next st] 10 times, k2.
5th row – [K11, inc in next st] 10 times, k2.
7th row – [K12, inc in next st] 10 times, k2.
9th row – [K13, inc in next st] 10 times, k2.   *152 sts.*
Work straight in st st until work measures 7cm/3 in from beg, ending after a p row.

Shape crown thus:
1st row – [K13, k2 tog] 10 times, k2.
2nd and alternate rows – P.
3rd row – [K12, k2 tog] 10 times, k2.
5th row – [K11, k2 tog] 10 times, k2.
Continue in this way decreasing 10 sts on every k row until 22 sts remain. Purl 1 row. Break yarn and thread through sts, draw up and fasten off.

PEAK
With 4 mm needles, cast on 40 sts.
1st row – K26, turn.
2nd row – Sl 1, p11, turn.
3rd row – Sl 1, k13, turn.
4th row – Sl 1, p15, turn.
5th row – Sl 1, k17, turn.
6th row – Sl 1, p19, turn.
Continue in this way, working 2 more sts on every row until the row 'Sl 1, p35, turn' has been worked.
Next row – Sl 1, k to end.
Next row – P to end.
Next row – K.
Next row – P.

Shape second side of peak thus:
1st row – K to last 2 sts, turn.
2nd row – Sl 1, p to last 2 sts, turn.
3rd row – Sl 1, k to last 4 sts, turn.
4th row – Sl 1, p to last 4 sts, turn.
Continue in this way, working 2 sts fewer on every row until the row 'Sl 1, p11, turn' has been worked.
Next row – Sl 1, k to end.
Next row – P to end.
Cast off.

TO MAKE UP
Press, following pressing instructions on ball band. Join side edges of main part. With k side outside, fold peak in half, bringing cast-on and cast-off edges together. Tack together and stitch the double edges to centre front section of main part, easing on peak. Cut petersham to fit head, allowing approx 2 cm/1 in for overlap. Overlapping side edges of petersham, sew one long edge of petersham to inside edge of headband of main part. Press seam and double outer edge of peak, slightly stretching outer edge. Sew button to top of crown.

PETER RABBIT
ROUND-YOKE CARDIGAN AND TONING STRIPED RIBBED SKIRT

I am sorry to say that Peter was not very well during the evening. His mother put him to bed, and made some camomile tea; and she gave a dose of it to Peter!

THE TALE OF PETER RABBIT

MEASUREMENTS
CARDIGAN

To fit chest	61	66	71	cm
	24	26	28	in
Length at centre back	39	43	47	cm
excluding neckband, approx	15½	17	18½	in
Sleeve seam	25	30	36	cm
	10	12	14	in

SKIRT

Length excluding	30	37	43	cm
waistband	12	14½	17	in

MATERIALS
Patons Diploma DK or Patons Clansman DK, 50 g balls
CARDIGAN

Main (M)	5	6	6

1 ball each White (A), Brown (B) and Green (C)
SKIRT

Main (M)	1	2	2
White (A)	1	1	2

2 balls each Brown (B) and Green (C)
A pair each 4 mm / No 8, 3¾ mm / No 9 and 3¼ mm / No 10 long needles. 9 buttons. Length of elastic for Skirt waist.

TENSION
22 sts and 30 rows to 10 cm / 4 in over plain st st on 4 mm / No 8 needles. 23 sts and 31 rows to 10 cm / 4 in over st st on 3¾ mm / No 9 needles.

ABBREVIATIONS
K = knit; kb = k into back of next st; p = purl; sts = stitches; st st = stocking st; inc = increase, increasing; dec = decrease, decreasing; tog = together; tbl = through back of loops; beg = beginning; rep = repeat; cm = centimetres; in = inches; M = Blue; A = White; B = Brown; C = Green.

CARDIGAN

SLEEVES
With 3¼ mm needles and M, cast on 35(37, 39) sts.
1st row (right side) – K1, [kb, p1] to last 2 sts, kb, k1.
2nd row – K1, [p1, k1] to end.
Work 16(20, 22) more rows in rib, inc 7 sts evenly on last row.   *42(44, 46) sts.*

Change to **4 mm needles** and, beg with a k row, work in st st, shaping sleeve by inc 1 st at each end of 3rd row, then on every following 8th(9th, 9th) row until there are 56(60, 64) sts. Work 7(4, 5) rows straight, thus ending after a p row.

Shape top thus:
1st and 2nd rows – Cast off 3 sts, work to end.
3rd row – K2, k2 tog tbl, k to last 4 sts, k2 tog, k2.
4th row – K1, p to last st, k1.
Rep 3rd and 4th rows until 42(44, 46) sts remain. Slip sts on a spare needle.

FRONTS AND BACK (worked in one piece up to armholes)
With 3¼ mm needles and M, cast on 143(155, 167) sts. Work 17(21, 23) rows in rib as on sleeves.
Next row – Rib 9(2, 8), *inc in next st, rib 4(5, 5); rep from * to last 9(3, 9) sts, inc in next st, rib to end.   *169(181, 193) sts.*

Change to **4 mm needles** and, beg with a k row, work 2 rows in st st. (N B. A third 4 mm needle may be used to hold sts on border if required.) Join in and break off colours as required. On two-colour rows carry colour not in use loosely across back of work over not more than 4 sts at a time.
Continue in st st and **work rabbit border** thus:
1st row – 3M, [1C, 5M] to last 4 sts, 1C, 3M.
2nd row – 2M, [3C, 3M] to last 5 sts, 3C, 2M.
3rd row – 2C, [3M, 3C] to last 5 sts, 3M, 2C.
4th row – 1C, [11M, 1C] to end.
5th row – 4M, [2B, 1A, 2B, 7M] to last 9 sts, 2B, 1A, 2B, 4M.
6th row – 3M, [2B, 3A, 2B, 5M] to last 10 sts, 2B, 3A, 2B, 3M.
7th and 8th rows – 2M, [3B, 3A, 3B, 3M] to last 11 sts, 3B, 3A, 3B, 2M.
9th row – 2M, [4B, 1A, 4B, 3M] to last 11 sts, 4B, 1A, 4B, 2M.
10th and 11th rows – 2M, [9B, 3M] to last 11 sts, 9B, 2M.
12th row – 3M, [7B, 5M] to last 10 sts, 7B, 3M.
13th and 14th rows – 4M, [5B, 7M] to last 9 sts, 5B, 4M.
15th row – 5M, [3B, 9M] to last 8 sts, 3B, 5M.
16th row – As 13th.
17th and 18th rows – As 12th.
19th row – As 13th.
20th row – As 15th.
21st row – As 13th.
22nd to 24th rows – 4M, [2B, 1M, 2B, 7M] to last 9 sts, 2B, 1M, 2B, 4M.
25th row – 5M, [1B, 1M, 1B, 9M] to last 8 sts, 1B, 1M, 1B, 5M.

Continue in M only. P 1 row.
Next row – K9(2, 8), *k2 tog, k4(5, 5); rep from * to last 10(4, 10) sts, k2 tog, k to end.   *143(155, 167) sts.*
Continue in st st until work measures 23(24, 26) cm / 9¼(9¾, 10¼) in from beg, ending after a k row.

Shape armholes thus:
Next row – P32(35, 38), cast off 6 sts, p to last 38(41, 44) sts, cast off 6 sts, p to end. Continue on last group for right front.
Next row – K to last 4 sts, k2 tog, k2.
Next row – K1, p to end. Rep these 2 rows until 28(30, 32) sts remain. Slip sts on a spare needle.

With right side facing, rejoin M to centre group of 67(73, 79) sts.
Next row – K2, k2 tog tbl, k to last 4 sts, k2 tog, k2.
Next row – K1, p to last st, k1.
Rep last 2 rows until 59(63, 67) sts remain. Slip sts on a spare needle.

With right side facing, rejoin M to remaining sts.
Next row – K2, k2 tog tbl, k to end.
Next row – P to last st, k1.
Rep last 2 rows until 28(30, 32) sts remain. P 1 row, inc 4 sts evenly. Leave sts on needle.

Work yoke thus:
Next row – With wrong side of each piece facing and M, using needle holding 32(34, 36) sts of left front, p across sts of left sleeve inc 1 st at centre, p across sts of back inc 8 sts evenly, p across sts of right sleeve inc 1 st at centre, finally p across sts of right front, inc 4 sts evenly.   *217(229, 241) sts.* (NB. A third 4 mm needle may be used to hold sts until number is reduced.)
Continue in st st, **working rabbit border** thus:
1st to 12th rows – As at commencement.
13th row – 4M, [5B, 2M, k2 tog M, 3M] to last 9 sts, 5B, 4M.   *200(211, 222) sts.*
14th row – 4M, [5B, 6M] to last 9 sts, 5B, 4M.
15th row – 5M, [3B, 8M] to last 8 sts, 3B, 5M.
16th row – As 14th.
17th and 18th rows – 3M, [7B, 4M] to last 10 sts, 7B, 3M.
19th row – 4M, [5B, 6M] to last 9 sts, 5B, 4M.
20th row – 1M, p2 tog tbl M, 2M, [3B, then in M, p1, p2 tog, p2, p2 tog tbl, p1] to last 8 sts, 3B, 2M, p2 tog M, 1M.   *164(173, 182) sts.*
21st row – 3M, [5B, 4M] to last 8 sts, 5B, 3M.
22nd to 24th rows – 3M, [2B, 1M, 2B, 4M] to last 8 sts, 2B, 1M, 2B, 3M.
25th row – 4M, [1B, 1M, 1B, 6M] to last 7 sts, 1B, 1M, 1B, 4M. Continue in M only.
26th row – P.
27th row – K1, [k2 tog, k1] to last st, kl.   *110(116, 122) sts.*
Work 4(10, 10) rows straight.

1st size only
Next row – P4, [p2 tog] 51 times, p4.   *59 sts.*

2nd size only
Next row – P5, [p2, tog] 53 times, p5.   *63 sts.*

3rd size only
Next row – P5, [p2 tog, p8] 11 times, p2 tog, p5.   *110 sts.*
Work 5 rows.
Next row – P3, *[p2 tog] 3 times, p1; rep from * to last 2 sts, p2.   *65 sts.*

All sizes
Change to 3¼ mm needles and work 8 rows in rib as on sleeves. Cast off in rib.

BORDERS
With 3¼ mm needles and M, cast on 9 sts. Work a strip in rib as on sleeves to fit up front edge, allowing for rib to be slightly stretched. Cast off firmly in rib. Mark position on border for 9 buttons, 1st to be in 3rd/4th rows, 3rd level with top of welt, 2nd spaced evenly between 1st and 3rd, 9th to be in 3rd/4th rows from top and remaining 5 spaced evenly between 3rd and 9th.

Work a second border as the first, but working holes to match markers thus:
1st row – Rib 3, cast off 3 sts in rib, rib to end.
2nd row – In rib, casting on 3 sts over those cast off.

TO MAKE UP
Omitting ribbing, press, following pressing instructions on ball band. Join shapings and sleeve seams. Sew on borders and buttons. Press seams.

SKIRT

BACK AND FRONT (2 pieces alike)
With 3¾ mm needles and B, cast on 155(164, 173) sts.
1st row (right side) – In B, k.
2nd row – In B, p2, [k7, p2] to end.
3rd row – In B, k2, [p7, k2] to end.
4th and 5th rows – As 2nd and 3rd.
6th row – As 2nd.
7th to 10th rows – In M, as 1st to 4th.
11th to 16th rows – In C, as 1st to 6th.
17th to 20th rows – In A, as 1st to 4th.
These 20 rows form basic striped rib. Work 24(34, 44) more rows.

Keeping rib and stripes correct, shape thus:
1st dec row – K2, [p2 tog, p3, p2 tog, k2] to end.   *121(128, 135) sts.*
Next row – P2, [k5, p2] to end.
Keeping rib and stripes correct, work 38(48, 48) rows straight.
2nd dec row – K2, [p2 tog, p1, p2 tog, k2] to end.   *87(92, 97) sts.*
Next row – P2, [k3, p2] to end.

Keeping rib and stripes correct, continue straight until work measures 30(37, 43) cm / 12(14½, 17) in from beg, ending after a right-side row. Break A, B and C. Continue in M.
Next row – P2(6, 10), [p2 tog, p1] 28(27, 26) times, p to end.   *59(65, 71) sts.*

Change to 3¼ mm needles and work 7 rows in rib as on Cardigan sleeves.
Cast off *very loosely* in rib.

TO MAKE UP
Do not press. Join side seams. Cut elastic to fit waist; join in a ring and sew inside waist ribbing using a herringbone stitch over the elastic to form a casing. Press seams, following pressing instructions on ball band.

SQUIRREL NUTKIN
COAT AND HAT

The other squirrels hunted up and down the nut bushes; but Nutkin gathered robin's pin-cushions off a briar bush, and stuck them full of pine-needle pins.

THE TALE OF SQUIRREL NUTKIN

MEASUREMENTS
COAT

To fit chest	61	66	71	cm
	24	26	28	in
Length at centre back,	60	69	77	cm
adjustable	23½	27	30½	in
Sleeve seam, adjustable	25	30	36	cm
	10	12	14	in

HAT

To fit a child aged approx	3–5	5–7	7–10

MATERIALS
For the set

Lister Machine Washable			
Aran (M), 40 g balls	11	13	15
Lister Shimmer Tweed (C),			
25 g balls	4	5	5

An oddment of green mohair or Aran for nut.
A pair each 5 mm/No 6 and 4 mm/No 8 needles. 6 buttons.
An oddment of black embroidery thread.

TENSION
18 sts and 22 rows to 10 cm/4 in over st st using M and 5 mm/No 6 needles.

ABBREVIATIONS
K = knit; p = purl; sts = stitches; st st = stocking st; g st = garter st; inc = increase, increasing; dec = decrease, decreasing; tog = together; tbl = through back of loops; beg = beginning; rep = repeat; mlp = make loops thus: insert right needle into next st as if to knit, wrap yarn over crossed points (working away from you) and over first finger of left hand 3 times, now bring yarn over point of right needle in usual way (as if to knit) and knit a loop through the 3 strands and st on left needle, slipping all 3 loops thus formed at back of work and original st off left needle, still leaving finger in loops; finally slip st on right needle back on to left needle and k firmly into back of it and withdraw finger from loops; alt = alternate; cm = centimetres; in = inches.

COAT

BACK
With 4 mm needles and M, cast on 81(88, 96) sts. Work 4 rows in g st.
Next row – K4(1, 5), [inc in next st, k11] 6(7, 7) times, inc in next st, k to end.   *88(96, 104) sts.*

Change to 5 mm needles and, beg with a k row, work 10(10, 12) rows in st st.

Shape thus:
Dec row – K10, *k2 tog tbl, k8(10, 12), k2 tog*, k to last 22(24, 26) sts, work from * to *, k10. (4 sts decreased.)
Work 13 rows straight. Rep the last 14 rows until 64(68, 72) sts remain. Work straight until back measures 43(51, 58) cm/17(20, 23) in at centre (or desired length), ending after a p row.

Shape raglan thus:
1st and 2nd rows – Cast off 3 sts, work to end.
3rd row – K1, k2 tog tbl, k to last 3 sts, k2 tog, k1.
4th row – K1, p2 tog, p to last 3 sts, p2 tog tbl, k1.
5th row – As 3rd.
6th row – K1, p to last st, k1.
Rep 5th and 6th rows only until 22(24, 24) sts remain, ending after a 6th row. Cast off *firmly*.

POCKET LININGS (2)
With 5 mm needles and M, cast on 21(23, 25) sts. Beg with a k row, work 22(24, 26) rows in st st. Slip sts on a spare needle.

RIGHT FRONT
With 4 mm needles and M, cast on 39(43, 47) sts. Work 5 rows in g st, inc 4 sts evenly on last row.   *43(47, 51) sts.*

Change to 5 mm needles and, beg with a k row, work 10(10, 12) rows in st st.**

Next row – K to last 6(9, 12) sts, k2 tog, k to end.   *42(46, 50) sts.*
Purl 1 row.
Working from Chart 5, and twisting yarns on wrong side when changing colours, continue in st st thus:
1st row – K, 11(12, 13)M, work 1st row of Chart 5, working from right to left, 5(8, 11)M.
2nd row – P, 5(8, 11)M, work 2nd row of Chart 5, working from left to right, 11(12, 13)M.
3rd to 12th rows – Rep 1st and 2nd rows 5 times, but working rows 3 to 12 of Chart 5.
13th row – Keeping chart correct, k to last 6(9, 12) sts, k2 tog, k to end.   *41(45, 49) sts.*
14th row – P, 4(7, 10)M, work 14th row of Chart 5, working from left to right, 11(12, 13)M.
15th to 26th rows – Keeping chart correct, work 12 rows straight.
27th row – As 13th row   *40(44, 48) sts.*
28th row – P, 3(6, 9)M, work 28th row of Chart 5, working from left to right, 11(12, 13)M.
29th to 34th rows – Keeping chart correct, work 6 rows straight. Continue in M only for remainder.
Next row – K.
Next row – P, dec 3 sts evenly.   *37(41, 45) sts.*

1st size only
Work 8 rows straight. **Place pocket** thus:
Next row – K10, *slip next 21 sts on a length of yarn and in place of these k across a group of lining sts, k to end. Work 9 rows straight.
Dec row – K to last 22 sts, k2 tog tbl, k8, k2 tog, k10. Work 13 rows straight. Rep dec row again.   *33 sts.*

2nd and 3rd sizes only
Work 18 rows straight.
Dec row – K to last 24(26) sts, k2 tog tbl, k 10(12), k2 tog, k10. Work 1(11) rows straight.
Place pocket thus:
Next row – K 10(12), *slip next 23(25) sts on a length of yarn and in place of these k across a group of lining sts, k to end.
Work 11(1) rows straight. Continue repeating dec row on next and every following 14th row until 35(37) sts remain.

***All sizes
Work straight until front measures same as back to raglan shaping, ending after a p row, and dec 2 sts evenly across on last row.   *31(33, 35) sts.****
K 1 row.

Shape raglan thus:
1st row – Cast off 3 sts, p to end.
2nd row – K to last 3 sts, k2 tog, k1.
3rd row – K1, p2 tog, p to end.
4th row – As 2nd.
5th row – K1, p to end.
Rep 4th and 5th rows only until 20(22, 22) sts remain.
Next row – K1, p to end.

****Shape neck** thus:
Continue dec at raglan edge as before, and dec at neck edge also on every k row until 4 sts remain. Continue dec at raglan edge only as before until 2 sts remain. Work 1 row. Fasten off.

LEFT FRONT
Work as right front to **.
Next row – K4(7, 10), k2 tog tbl, k to end.   *42(46, 50) sts.*
Purl 1 row.

Continue in st st, **working from Chart 5** thus:
1st row – K, 5(8, 11)M, work 1st row of Chart 5, working from left to right, 11(12, 13)M.
2nd row – P, 11(12, 13)M, work 2nd row of Chart 5, working from right to left, 5(8, 11)M.
3rd to 12th rows – As right front.
13th row – K 4(7, 10), k2 tog tbl, keeping chart correct, k to end.   *41(45, 49) sts.*
14th to 26th rows – Keeping chart correct, work 13 rows straight.
27th row – As 13th row.   *40(44, 48) sts.*
28th to 34th rows – Keeping chart correct, work 7 rows straight. Continue in M only for remainder.
Next row – K.
Next row – P, dec 3 sts evenly.   *37(41, 45) sts.*

1st size only
Work 8 rows straight. **Place pocket** thus:
Next row – K6, work as right front pocket row from * to end. Work 9 rows straight.
Dec row – K10, k2 tog tbl, k8, k2 tog, k to end. Work 13 rows straight. Rep dec row again.   *33 sts.*

CHART 5

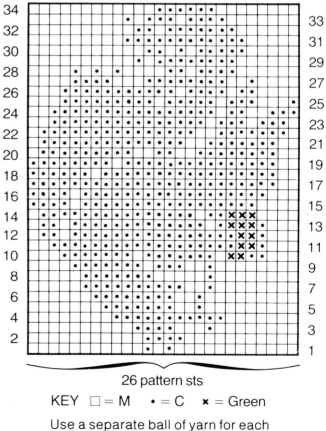

26 pattern sts

KEY   □ = M   • = C   × = Green

Use a separate ball of yarn for each colour area where possible, otherwise carry colour not in use *loosely* over not more than 3 sts at a time.

2nd and 3rd sizes only
Work 18 rows straight.
Dec row – K10, k2 tog tbl, k 10(12), k2 tog, k to end.
Work 1(11) rows straight. **Place pocket** thus:
Next row – K6, work as right front pocket row from * to end.
Work 11(1) rows straight. Continue repeating dec row on next and every following 14th row until 35(37) sts remain.

All sizes
Work as right front from *** to ***.

Shape raglan thus:
1st row – Cast off 3 sts, k to end.
2nd row – P to last st, k1.
3rd row – K1, k2 tog tbl, k to end.
4th row – P to last 3 sts, p2 tog tbl, k1.
5th row – As 3rd.
6th row – As 2nd.
Rep 5th and 6th rows only until 20(22, 22) sts remain.
Next row – P to last st, k1.
Complete as right front, working from **** to end.

SLEEVES
With 4 mm needles and M, cast on 27(29, 31) sts loosely.
Work 14 rows in g st.
Next row (hem) – Fold work in half to wrong side and k each st on needle tog with corresponding loop from cast-on edge.
Next row – K4, inc in next 18(20, 22) sts, k5.   *45(49, 53) sts.*

Change to 5 mm needles and, beg with a k row, work in st st until sleeve measures 25(30, 36) cm / 10(12, 14) in from lower edge (or desired length), ending after a p row.

Shape raglan thus:
1st to 3rd rows – As on back.
4th row – K1, p to last st, k1.
Rep 3rd and 4th rows until 5(7, 7) sts remain.
Next row – P1(2, 2), p3 tog, p1(2, 2). Cast off.

POCKET TOPS
With right side facing, slip a group of pocket sts on to a 4 mm needle. Join in M and, noting that 1st row will be right side, work 7 rows in g st. Cast off.

BORDERS (2 pieces alike)
First join raglan shapings. **With 5 mm needles and C,** cast on 9 sts.

1st row (right side) – K.
2nd row – K1, [mlp, k1] 4 times.
3rd row – K, working into back of sts.
4th and 5th rows – K.
6th row – K2, [mlp, k1] 3 times, k1.
7th row – As 3rd.
8th row – K.
Rep these 8 rows until strip fits up front edge and round to centre back of neck. Cast off loosely.

TO MAKE UP
Embroider eyes and whiskers with black embroidery thread. Omitting borders, press, following pressing instructions on Listers Aran ball band. Sew down pocket linings on wrong side and tops on right side. Join side and sleeve seams. Join cast-off edges of border. With right side of border to wrong side of main part sew border in position all round, stretching border well around neck. Fold border to right side and hem in position. Work 6 buttonhole loops evenly spaced along right front edge, commencing at neck shaping. Sew on buttons to left front to correspond.

HAT

With 4 mm needles and M, cast on 73(76, 79) sts. Work 5 rows in g st, inc 4 sts evenly on last row.   *77(80, 83) sts.*

Change to 5 mm needles and, beg with a k row, work 24 rows in st st, dec 4(7, 10) sts evenly on last row.   *73 sts.*

Shape crown thus:
1st row – [K7, k2 tog] 8 times, k1.
2nd and alt rows – P.
3rd row – [K6, k2 tog] 8 times, k1.
5th row – [K5, k2 tog] 8 times, k1.
Continue in this way, dec 8 sts on every following k row until 17 sts remain. Break yarn. Run end through sts, draw up and fasten off. Join seam.

Now work one strip as for Coat borders to measure 43(44, 46) cm / 17(17½, 18) in not stretched, ending after a 3rd or 7th row. Cast off loosely.
Join short ends of border. Sew border to hat, allowing for border to fold over to right side.

MRS. TITTLEMOUSE
CHILD'S JERKIN AND WAISTCOAT, WITH LADYBIRD AND BABBITTY BUMBLE BEE MOTIFS

They went along the sandy passage – 'Tiddly widdly –' 'Buzz! Wizz! Wizz!'
He met Babbitty round a corner, and snapped her up, and put her down again.
THE TALE OF MRS. TITTLEMOUSE

MEASUREMENTS

To fit chest	61	66	71	76	81	86	cm
	24	26	28	30	32	34	in
Length from	33	38	46	53	56	58	cm
shoulder	13	15	18	21	22	23	in

MATERIALS

Sirdar Panorama D K, 50 g balls
JERKIN

Main shade (M)	5	5	5	6	6	6

An oddment each of Red, White, Black and Gold.
WAISTCOAT

Main (M)	5	5	6	6	7	7

An oddment each of White, Black and Gold.
A pair each 4 mm / No 8 and 3¼ mm / No 10 needles. 5(5, 5, 6, 6, 6) buttons for Waistcoat.

TENSION

24 sts and 30 rows to 10 cm/4 in over st st on 4 mm/No 8 needles.

ABBREVIATIONS

K = knit; p = purl; sts = stitches; st st = stocking st; inc = increase, increasing; dec = decrease, decreasing; tog = together; beg = beginning; alt = alternate; foll = following; cm = centimetres; in = inches; M = main shade.

JERKIN

BACK

With 3¼ mm needles and M, cast on 69(75, 81, 87, 93, 99) sts.
1st row (right side) – K2, [p1, k1] to last st, k1.
2nd row – K1, [p1, k1] to end.
Work 22(22, 26, 26, 30, 30) more rows in rib, inc 11 sts evenly on last row.   *80(86, 92, 98, 104, 110) sts.***

Change to 4 mm needles and, beg with a k row, work 74(90, 108, 130, 134, 142) rows in st st.

Shape shoulders thus:
Cast off 9(10, 10, 11, 11, 12) sts at beg of next 4 rows, then 9(9, 11, 10, 12, 12) sts at beg of next 2 rows. Slip final 26(28, 30, 34, 36, 38) sts on a spare needle.

POCKET LININGS (2)

With 4 mm needles and M, cast on 23(25, 27, 29, 31, 33) sts. Beg with a k row, work 20(24, 26, 32, 32, 36) rows in st st, p rows having k1 at each end. Slip sts on a spare needle.

FRONT

Work as back to **.

Change to 4 mm needles and, beg with a k row, work 20(24, 26, 32, 32, 36) rows in st st.

Place pocket linings thus:
Next row – K7, *slip next 23(25, 27, 29, 31, 33) sts on a spare needle and in place of these k across a group of lining sts*, k20(22, 24, 26, 28, 30), work from * to *, k7.
Continue in st st on all sts and work 11(21, 35, 45, 47, 45) rows. (N B. Variation in rows worked is controlled by the variable placing of the charts for the different sizes.)

Continue in st st, **working Ladybird from Chart 6** (see page 34) thus:
1st row – 32(35, 38, 41, 44, 47)M, work 1st row of chart, 32(35, 38, 41, 44, 47)M.
2nd to 6th rows – As 1st row, working rows 2 to 6 of Chart 6.

Work Babbitty Bumble Bee from Chart 7 (see page 34) thus:
1st row – 2(4, 6, 8, 10, 12)M, work 1st row of Chart 7, 4(5, 6, 7, 8, 9)M, work 7th row of Chart 6, 4(5, 6, 7, 8, 9)M, work 1st row of Chart 7, 2(4, 6, 8, 10, 12)M.
2nd to 9th rows – Continue with charts as placed on last row, working rows 2 to 9 of Chart 7, and rows 8 to 15 of Chart 6. Working centre sts all in M and keeping Chart 7 correct, work 5(7, 9, 11, 13, 15) rows noting that, on 4th, 5th and 6th sizes only, when Chart 7 is complete all sts should be worked in M.

Shape neck thus (N B. On 1st, 2nd and 3rd sizes only, when Chart 7 is complete all sts should be worked in M):
Next row – K32(34, 36, 37, 39, 41), turn.
Continue on this group. Dec 1 st at neck edge on next 2 rows, then on the 3 foll alt rows.   *27(29, 31, 32, 34, 36) sts.*
***Work straight until front measures same as back to shoulder shaping, ending at side edge.

Shape shoulder by casting off 9(10, 10, 11, 11, 12) sts at beg of next and foll alt row. Work 1 row. Cast off.***

32

With right side facing, slip centre 16(18, 20, 24, 26, 28) sts on a spare needle. Rejoin yarn(s) and k 1 row. Complete as first side.

POCKET TOPS

Slip a group of pocket sts on to a 3¼ mm needle. Join in M and, noting that 1st row will be right side, work 5(5, 6, 6, 7, 7) rows in rib as on welt. Cast off evenly in rib.

NECKBAND

First join left shoulder. **With 3¼ mm needles and M**, right side facing, k up 91(95, 99, 111, 115, 125) sts evenly round neck, including sts on spare needles. Beg with a 2nd row, work 6(6, 7, 7, 8, 8) rows in rib as on welt. Cast off evenly in rib, working *loosely* on first 3 sizes.

(continued over page)

ARMBANDS

First join right shoulder and neckband. **Place a marker 38(42, 46, 52, 56, 60) rows down from each shoulder on all edges. With 3¼ mm needles and M**, right side facing, k up 67(73, 81, 89, 95, 103) sts evenly between 1 set of markers. Beg with a 2nd row, work 6(6, 7, 7, 8, 8) rows in rib as on welt. Cast off evenly in rib.

TO MAKE UP

First embroider legs and feelers in black on the insects. Omitting ribbing, press, following pressing instructions on ball band. Sew down pocket tops on right side and linings on wrong side. Join side seams and edges of armbands.** Press seams.

WAISTCOAT

BACK

Work as back of Jerkin, but casting off final sts.

POCKET LININGS (2)

Work as for Jerkin.

RIGHT FRONT

With 3¼ mm needles and M, cast on 35(39, 41, 45, 47, 51) sts. Work 24(24, 28, 28, 32, 32) rows in rib as on back, inc 4(3, 4, 3, 4, 3) sts evenly on last row.   39(42, 45, 48, 51, 54) sts.

Change to 4 mm needles and, beg with a k row, work 20(24, 26, 32, 32, 36) rows in st st.

Place pocket lining thus:
Next row – K9(10, 11, 12, 13, 14), *slip next 23(25, 27, 29, 31, 33) sts on a spare needle and in place of these k across a group of lining sts, k to end.
Work 11(19, 31, 43, 43, 43) rows.

Shape front slope thus:
Dec 1 st at front edge on next row, then on every alt row until

35(38, 38, 39, 42, 45) sts remain. Work 1(1, 3, 3, 3, 3) rows straight.

Place Chart 7 thus:
Next row – K2 tog M, k5(7, 6, 6, 8, 10)M, work 1st row of chart, k2(3, 4, 5, 6, 7)M.
Continue working rows 2 to 19 of Chart 7 as placed on last row, *at the same time* dec 1 st at front edge on every foll 4th row until 27(29, 31, 32, 34, 36) sts remain, noting that when 19th row of chart has been worked all sts should be worked in M.
Work as front of Jerkin from *** to ***.

LEFT FRONT

Noting that pocket row will be 'K7, work as right front pocket row from * to end', work as right front up to row placing chart.
Place Chart 7 thus:
Next row – K2(3, 4, 5, 6, 7)M, work 1st row of Chart 7, k to last 2 sts in M, k2 tog M.
Complete to match right front.

POCKET TOPS AND ARMBANDS

Work pocket tops as Jerkin. Join shoulders. Work armbands as for Jerkin, working from ** to end.

BORDERS

With 3¼ mm needles and M, cast on 11 sts. Work a strip in rib to fit up front edge and round to centre back of neck when border is slightly stretched. Cast off in rib. Mark position on border for 5(5, 5, 6, 6, 6) buttons, the first one to be in 3rd/4th rows, last one level with or a few rows below start of front slope, and remainder spaced evenly between.
Work a second strip as first, working holes to match markers thus:
1st row – Rib 4, cast off 3 sts in rib, rib to end.
2nd row – In rib, casting on 3 over those cast off.

TO MAKE UP

Make up as Jerkin to **. Sew on borders, joining ends at back of neck. Sew on buttons. Press seams.

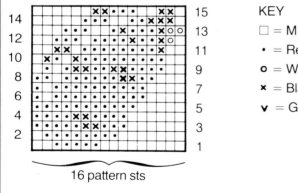

CHART 6

KEY

☐ = M
• = Red
o = White
✕ = Black
v = Gold

Read odd rows k from right to left and even rows p from left to right.

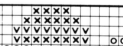

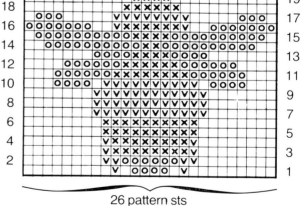

CHART 7

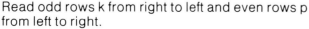

26 pattern sts

Use small balls of yarn for each colour area where possible, twisting yarns on wrong side when changing colour.

MRS. TITTLEMOUSE
EMBROIDERED PARTY DRESS

Once upon a time there was a wood-mouse, and her name was Mrs. Tittlemouse.

THE TALE OF MRS. TITTLEMOUSE

MEASUREMENTS

To fit chest					
	56	61	66	71	cm
	22	24	26	28	in
Length from shoulder	43	51	58	69	cm
(adjustable)	17	20	23	27	in
Sleeve seam (adjustable)	23	27	30	36	cm
	9	10½	12	14	in

MATERIALS

Lister Motoravia 4 ply, 50 g balls

White (M)	2	3	3	3
1st contrast (A)	2	2	2	3
2nd contrast (B)	2	3	3	3

A pair each 3¼ mm/No 10 and 2¾ mm/No 12 needles. Approx 1.5 m narrow white ribbon. 3 small buttons.

TENSION

28 sts and 36 rows to 10 cm/4 in over st st on 3¼ mm/No 10 needles.

ABBREVIATIONS

K = knit; p = purl; sts = stitches; patt = pattern; st st = stocking st; inc = increase, increasing; dec = decrease, decreasing; beg = beginning; alt = alternate; rep = repeat; foll = following; yrn = yarn round needle; tog = together; cm = centimetres; in = inches.

FRONT

With 2¾ mm needles and M, cast on 140(151, 162, 173) sts loosely. K3 rows.
Next row – K4(5, 5, 6), [inc in next st, k9] 13(14, 15, 16) times, inc in next st, k to end.   *154(166, 178, 190) sts.*

Change to 3¼ mm needles and patt thus:
1st to 3rd rows – In A, beg with a k row, work 3 rows in st st.
4th row – In A, p55(61, 67, 73), [p2 tog, yrn, p8] 5 times, p to end.
5th to 7th rows – As 1st to 3rd.
8th row – P, [1A, 1M] to end.
9th to 12th rows – In M, beg with a k row, work 4 rows in st st.

13th to 15th rows – In B as 1st to 3rd.
16th row – In B, p60(66, 72, 78), [p2 tog, yrn, p8] 4 times, p to end.
17th to 20th rows – In B as 5th to 8th, but using B in place of A on 20th row.
21st to 24th rows – As 9th to 12th.
These 24 rows form striped patt with centre eyelet holes.

Continue in patt until work measures 31(37, 43, 52) cm/ 12¼(14¾, 17¼, 20¾) in from beg, ending after a wrong-side row. (N B. Length may be adjusted here.)

Keeping patt correct, **shape armholes** thus:
Cast off 6(8, 10, 12) sts at beg of next 2 rows. Dec 1 st at each end of next 5(7, 7, 9) rows, then on the 3 foll alt rows.   *126(130, 138, 142) sts.*
Work 1 row. Break M and A. Continue in B.
Next row – K3(7, 7, 11), [k2 tog] 4(2, 2, 4) times, [k3 tog, k2 tog, k2 tog] 16(16, 17, 16) times, k to end.   *58(64, 68, 74) sts.*
Next row – P.

Work eyelets for ribbon thus:
1st row – K8, yarn forward, k2 tog through back of loops, k to last 10 sts, k2 tog, yarn forward, k8.
Work 3 rows in st st.
These 4 rows form yoke patt.**
Continue in patt until work measures 8(9, 9, 10) cm/3¼ (3½, 3¾, 4) in from beg of armhole shaping, ending after a p row.

Keeping eyelets correct, **shape neck** thus:
Next row – Work across 20(22, 23, 25) sts, turn. Continue on this group. Dec 1 st at neck edge on next 5 rows.   *15(17, 18, 20) sts.*
Work straight until front measures 43(51, 58, 69) cm/17(20, 23, 27) in from beg, ending at armhole edge.

Shape shoulder thus: Cast off 5(6, 6, 7) sts at beg of next and foll alt row. Work 1 row. Cast off.

With right side facing, slip centre 18(20, 22, 24) sts on a spare needle. Rejoin B to remaining sts. K 1 row. Complete as first side.

BACK
Work as front to **. Patt 8 more rows.

Divide for neck opening thus:
Next row – Work across 29(32, 34, 37), turn.
Continue on this group. Working 4 sts at inner edge in garter st and remainder as before, work straight until back measures same as front to shoulder shaping, ending at armhole edge.

Shape shoulder thus:
Cast off 5(6, 6, 7) sts at beg of next and foll alt row, then 5(5, 6, 6) sts at beg of foll alt row. Work 1 row. Slip final 14(15, 16, 17) sts on a spare needle. Rejoin B to remaining sts and complete as first side.

SLEEVES
With 2¾ mm needles and B, cast on 41(45, 47, 51) sts.
1st row (right side) – K2, [p1, k1] to last st, k1.
2nd row – K1, [p1, k1] to end.
Work 15(19, 23, 23) more rows in rib.
Next row – Rib 4(4, 2, 3), [inc once in each of next 2 sts, rib 1] 11(12, 14, 15) times, inc in next st, rib to end.   *64(70, 76, 82) sts.*

Change to 3¼ mm needles and work rows 1 to 24 of patt as on front, *but* noting that 4th row will be: In A, p20(23, 26, 29), [p2 tog, yrn, p8] 3 times, p to end, and that 16th row will be: In B, p25(28, 31, 34), [p2 tog, yrn, p8] twice, p to end.

Continue in patt, **shaping sleeve** by inc 1 st at each end of next and every foll 6th (6th, 6th, 8th) row until there are 76(84, 92, 100) sts.
Work straight until sleeve measures 23(27, 30, 36) cm/

9(10½, 12, 14) in from beg, ending after a wrong-side row. (N B. Length may be adjusted here.)

Shape top thus:
Cast off 6(8, 10, 12) sts at beg of next 2 rows. Work 1(3, 5, 7) rows straight. Dec 1 st at each end of every p row until 54 sts remain, then on every row until 44 sts remain. Cast off.

NECKBAND
First join shoulders. **With 2¾ mm needles and M**, right side facing, k across left back sts dec 2 sts evenly, k up 11(13, 14, 16) sts down left front neck, k across centre sts dec 5 sts evenly, k up 11(13, 14, 16) sts up right front neck, finally k across right back neck sts dec 2 sts evenly.   *59(67, 73, 81) sts.*
K4 rows.
Picot row – Cast off 3 sts, *slip st on right needle back on to left needle, cast on 3 sts, cast off 8 sts firmly; rep from * until no sts remain.

LOWER BORDER
With 2¾ mm needles and M, right side facing, k up 1 st from every cast-on st at lower edge of front. Work picot row as on neckband. Rep border on back.

TO MAKE UP
With M, embroider a six-petal lazy-daisy round each eyelet. Omitting cuffs, press, following pressing instructions on ball band. Join side and sleeve seams. Sew in sleeves, easing in tops to fit armholes. Press seams. Sew buttons equally spaced to one back neck edge, then work a loop to correspond with each on other edge. Cut ribbon into 4 equal lengths. Sew one end of each piece to wrong side at base of yoke, level with yoke eyelets. Now slot ribbon through eyelets, tying in a bow at shoulder.

EDWARDIAN LACE
GIRL'S PARTY SMOCK

*When it was all beautifully neat and clean, she gave a party to five other
little mice, without Mr. Jackson.*
THE TALE OF MRS. TITTLEMOUSE

MEASUREMENTS

To fit chest	66	71	76	81	86	cm
	26	28	30	32	34	in
Length from	49	54	60	63	66	cm
shoulder	19½	21½	23½	25	26	in
Sleeve seam	28	31	34	37	39	cm
excluding frill (adjustable)	11	12¼	13½	14¾	15½	in

MATERIALS

Twilleys Galaxia 3,

100 g balls	11	11	12	12	13

A pair each 4 mm/No 8 and 3¼ mm/No 10 long needles. A
cable needle. 2 small buttons. Length of ribbon (optional).
Shirring elastic.

TENSION

28 sts and 36 rows to 10 cm/4 in over st st on 3¼ mm/No 10
needles.

ABBREVIATIONS

K = knit; p = purl; sts = stitches; st st = stocking st; patt =
pattern; inc = increase, increasing; dec = decrease, decreasing; beg = beginning; alt = alternate; rep = repeat; foll =
following; yfwd = yarn forward; yrn = yarn round needle;
sl = slip; psso = pass slipped st over; tog = together; C B =
slip next 3 sts on cable needle to back of work, k3, now k3
from cable needle; C F = slip next 3 sts on cable needle to
front of work, k3, now k3 from cable needle; cm = centimetres; in = inches.

FRONT

With 3¼ mm needles, cast on 191(197, 203, 209, 215) sts. K 1
row.
Change to 4 mm needles and work in patt thus:
1st row (right side) – P10(13, 16, 19, 22), *k6, [yfwd, sl 1, k1,
psso] twice, k1, [k2 tog, yfwd] twice, k6, p9; rep from * to last
1(4, 7, 10, 13) sts, p to end.
2nd, 4th and 6th rows – K10(13, 16, 19, 22), [p21, k9] 6 times,
k1(4, 7, 10, 13).

3rd row – P4(7, 10, 13, 16), [yrn, p3 tog, yrn, p3, k7, yfwd,
sl 1, k1, psso, yfwd, sl 1, k2 tog, psso, yfwd, k2 tog, yfwd,
k7, p3] 6 times, yrn, p3 tog, yrn, p4(7, 10, 13, 16).
5th row – P2(5, 8, 11, 14), *p2 tog, yrn, p3, yrn, p2 tog, p1, k6,
[yfwd, sl l, k1, psso] twice, k1, [k2 tog, yfwd] twice, k6, p1;
rep from * to last 9(12, 15, 18, 21) sts, p2 tog, yrn, p3, yrn, p2
tog, p to end.
7th row – P4(7, 10, 13, 16), [yrn, p3 tog, yrn, p3, CB, k1,
yfwd, sl 1, K1, psso, yfwd, sl 1, k2 tog, psso, yfwd, k2 tog,
yfwd, k1, CF, p3] 6 times, yrn, p3 tog, yrn, p4(7, 10, 13, 16).
8th row – As 2nd.
These 8 rows form patt.
Continue in patt until work measures 36(39, 43, 46, 47)
cm/14(15½, 17, 18, 18½) in at centre when slightly stretched,
ending after a wrong-side row. Mark centre of last row.

Keeping patt correct, **shape square armholes** thus:
Cast off 15(16, 17, 18, 19) sts *very firmly* at beg of next 2
rows. *161(165, 169, 173, 177) sts.*
Working 1(3, 5, 7, 9) sts at each end of rows in st st, work 4(4,
6, 8, 8) rows.
Change to 3¼ mm needles.
Next row – K1, [k2 tog] to end. *81(83, 85, 87, 89) sts.*
Next row – P, dec 7(5, 5, 3, 1) sts evenly across. *74(78, 80,
84, 88) sts.***
Beg with a k row, work in st st until front measures 10(10, 11,
13, 13) cm/4(4, 4½, 5, 5) in from marker, ending after a k
row.

Shape neck thus:
Next row – P28(29, 29, 30, 31), cast off centre 18(20, 22, 24, 26)
sts, p to end. Continue on last group. Dec 1 st at neck edge
on next 5 rows. *23(24, 24, 25, 26) sts.*
Work 7(11, 11, 11, 15) rows straight. (NB. Work 1 row more
here on second side.)

Shape shoulder thus:
Cast off 8 sts at beg of next and foll alt row. Work 1 row. Cast
off.

With right side facing, rejoin yarn to remaining sts. Complete as first side.

BACK

Work as front to **. Beg with a k row, work in st st until back measures 17 rows less than front up to shoulder shaping, ending after a k row.

Next row – P34(36, 37, 39, 41), k6, p to end.

Divide for opening thus:

Next row – K37(39, 40, 42, 44), turn.

Continue on this group. Working 3 sts at inner edge in garter st, work 15 rows. (NB. Work 1 row more here on second side.)

Shape shoulder thus:

Cast off 8 sts at beg of next and foll alt row, then 7(8, 8, 9, 10) sts at beg of next alt row. Work 1 row. Cast off.

With right side facing, rejoin yarn to remaining sts. Complete as first side.

SLEEVES

With 4 mm needles, cast on 75(75, 87, 87, 87) sts loosely. K 1 row.

Work in patt thus:

1st row (right side) – K3, *[yfwd, sl 1, k1, psso] twice, k1, [k2 tog, yfwd] twice, k3; rep from * to end.

2nd row – K3, [p9, k3] to end.

3rd row – K4, [*yfwd, sl 1, k1, psso, yfwd, sl 1, k2 tog, psso, yfwd, k2 tog, yfwd*, k5] to last 11 sts, work from * to *, k4.

4th row – As 2nd.

Rep these 4 rows 4(4, 5, 6, 6) times more.

Next row – K4(6, 2, 4, 6), [k2 tog] 33(31, 41, 39, 37) times, k to end.   *42(44, 46, 48, 50) sts.*

Change to 3¼ mm needles and work 7 rows in k1, p1 rib.

Next row – K, inc once in every st.

Next row – P29(28, 30, 29, 31), [inc in next st, p2] 9(11, 11, 13, 13) times, p to end.   *93(99, 103, 109, 113) sts.*

Change to 4 mm needles and patt thus:

1st row (right side) – P3(6, 8, 11, 13), [yrn, p3 tog, yrn, p9] to last 6(9, 11, 14, 16) sts, yrn, p3 tog, yrn, p to end.

2nd and alt rows – K.

3rd row – P1(4, 6, 9, 11), [p2 tog, yrn, p3, yrn, p2 tog, p5] to last 8(11, 13, 16, 18) sts, p2 tog, yrn, p3, yrn, p2 tog, p to end.

5th row – As 1st.

7th row – P.

9th row – P9(12, 14, 5, 7), [yrn, p3 tog, yrn, p9] to last 12(15, 17, 8, 10) sts, yrn, p3 tog, yrn, p to end.

11th row – P7(10, 12, 3, 5), [p2 tog, yrn, p3, yrn, p2 tog, p5] to last 14(17, 19, 10, 12) sts, p2 tog, yrn, p3, yrn, p2 tog, p to end.

13th row – As 9th.

15th row – P.

16th row – K.

These 16 rows form patt.

Continue in patt until sleeve measures 28(31, 34, 37, 39) cm/11(12¼, 13½, 14¾, 15½) in from base of ribbing, when slightly stretched, ending after a k row. (Length may be adjusted here.) Mark each end of last row.

Patt 12(12, 14, 16, 16) rows. Mark each end of last row.

Keeping patt correct, **shape top** by casting off 4 sts at beg of next 16(18, 20, 20, 22) rows. Cast off.

COLLAR (2 pieces alike)

With 3¼ mm needles, cast on 45(48, 51, 54, 57) sts loosely. K 1 row.

Work in patt thus:

1st row – K3, *[yfwd, sl 1, k1, psso] twice, k1, [k2 tog, yfwd] twice**, k1(2, 3, 4, 5); rep from * to last 12 sts, work from * to **, k3.

2nd row – K3, *p9, k1(2, 3, 4, 5); rep from * to last 12 sts, p9, k3.

3rd row – K4, *yfwd, sl 1, k1, psso, yfwd, sl 1, k2 tog, psso, yfwd, k2 tog, yfwd**, k3(4, 5, 6, 7); rep from * to last 11 sts, work from * to **, k4.

4th row – As 2nd.

Rep these 4 rows 5(5, 6, 7, 7) times more. Cast off.

TO MAKE UP

Do not press. Join shoulders. Stitch shaped top edge of sleeves to straight section of armholes, easing in tops to fit; stitch marked sections of sleeves to armhole cast-offs. Join side and sleeve seams. Sew on collar pieces. Run 2–3 rows of shirring elastic through wrist ribbing, drawing up to fit wrist. Sew buttons to one back neck edge, then work a loop to correspond with each on other edge. Make a ribbon bow and stitch between collar pieces at front if desired.

PETER RABBIT
JOGGING SWEATER

*'Peter got down very quietly off the wheelbarrow,
and started running as fast as he could go . . .*
THE TALE OF PETER RABBIT

MEASUREMENTS

To fit chest	61	66	71	76	81	86 cm
	24	*26*	*28*	*30*	*32*	*34 in*
Actual width at	71	76	81	89	97	107 cm
underarms	*28*	*30*	*32*	*35*	*38*	*42 in*
Length from	42	46	49	53	57	58 cm
shoulder	*16½*	*18*	*19½*	*21*	*22½*	*23 in*
Sleeve seam	29	33	36	37	41	43 cm
(adjustable)	*11½*	*13*	*14*	*14½*	*16*	*17 in*

MATERIALS

Richard Poppleton Emmerdale D K, 50 g balls

Main (M)		4	4	5	6	7	7

1 ball (50 g) each Brown (A), Blue (B) and White (C).
A pair each 4 mm/No 8 and 3¼ mm/No 10 needles. Set of four 3¼ mm/No 10 needles. A few lengths of Anchor stranded cotton in black.

TENSION

24 sts and 32 rows to 10 cm/4 in over st st on 4 mm/No 8 needles.

ABBREVIATIONS

K = knit; p = purl; sts = stitches; st st = stocking st; inc = increase, increasing; dec = decrease, decreasing; beg = beginning; alt = alternate; foll = following; rep = repeat; cm = centimetres; in = inches; M = main shade; A = Brown; B = Blue; C = White.

FRONT

With 3¼ mm needles and M, cast on 73(79, 85, 93, 101, 109) sts.
1st row (right side) – In M, k2, [p1, k1] to last st, k1.
2nd row – In M, k1, [p1, k1] to end.
3rd to 8th rows – Rep 1st and 2nd rows 3 times but working 2 rows B, 2 rows C, 2 rows A.
Rep these 8 rows 1(1, 1, 2, 2, 2) times *more*, then 1st to 7th rows again.
Next row – In A, rib 3(6, 4, 2, 5, 9), *inc in next st, rib 5(5, 6, 7, 6, 5); rep from * to last 4(7, 4, 3, 5, 10) sts, inc in next st, rib to end.   *85(91, 97, 105, 115, 125) sts.*

Change to 4 mm needles and, beg with a k row, work 2(4, 12, 12, 14, 18) rows in st st.**
Continue in st st thus:

***Next row** – 1M, [1A, 1M] to end.
Next row – In M.
Now work from Chart 1 (see page 43) thus:
1st row – K, 55(59, 63, 68, 74, 80)M, work 1st row of chart, 13(15, 17, 20, 24, 28)M.
2nd row – P, 13(15, 17, 20, 24, 28)M, work 2nd row of chart, p to end in M.
3rd to 27th rows – Rep the last 2 rows 12 times, then 1st row again, but working rows 3 to 27 of Chart 1.***
Using M only, work 1(3, 5, 5, 7, 7) rows.

Next row – 1M, [1A, 1M] to end.
Next row – In M.
Now work from Chart 1 thus:
1st row – 13(15, 17, 20, 24, 28)M, work 1st row of chart, 55(59, 63, 68, 74, 80)M.
2nd row – 55(59, 63, 68, 74, 80)M, work 2nd row of chart, p to end in M.
3rd to 27th rows – Rep the last 2 rows 12 times, then 1st row again but working rows 3 to 27 of Chart 1.
Using M only, work 1(3, 5, 5, 7, 7) rows.

Work from *** to ***.
Continue in M only for remainder and work a few rows straight until front measures 38(41, 44, 47, 49, 51) cm/15(16, 17½, 18½, 19½, 20) in from beg, ending after a p row.

Shape neck thus:
Next row – K35(37, 39, 42, 46, 50), turn.
Continue on this group. Dec 1 st at neck edge on next 5 rows.   *30(32, 34, 37, 41, 45) sts.*
Work 6(10, 10, 14, 18, 18) rows straight thus ending at side edge.

Shape shoulder thus:
Cast off 10(10, 11, 12, 14, 15) sts at beg of next and foll alt row. Work 1 row. Cast off.

With right side facing, slip centre 15(17, 19, 21, 23, 25) sts on to a spare needle. Rejoin M and k 1 row. Complete as first side, working 1 row more before shaping shoulder.

BACK

Work as front to **.

Continue in st st thus:
Next row – 1M, (1A, 1M) to end.
Beg with a p row, work 29(31, 33, 33, 35, 35) rows. Rep the

last 30(32, 34, 34, 36, 36) rows twice more. Continue in M only until back measures same as front to shoulder shaping, ending after a p row.

Shape shoulders thus:
Cast off 10(10, 11, 12, 14, 15) sts at beg of next 4 rows, then 10(12, 12, 13, 13, 15) sts at beg of foll 2 rows. Slip final 25(27, 29, 31, 33, 35) sts on a spare needle.

RIGHT SLEEVE

With 3¼ mm needles and M, cast on 37(39, 41, 43, 45, 47) sts. Work 24(24, 24, 32, 32, 32) rows in striped ribbing as on front. Continue in M.
Next row – K1, (inc in next st, k1) to end.   *55(58, 61, 64, 67, 70) sts.*
Next row – P5(5, 8, 2, 10, 9), *inc in next st, p4(3, 2, 2, 1, 1); rep from * to last 5(5, 8, 2, 11, 9) sts, inc in next st, p to end.   *65(71, 77, 85, 91, 97) sts.*

Change to 4 mm needles and, beg with a k row, continue in st st and work 6(8, 10, 12, 14, 16) rows.
Next row – 1M, (1A, 1M) to end.
Next row – In M.

Now work from Chart 1 thus:
1st row – K, 24(27, 30, 34, 37, 40)M, work 1st row of chart, 24(27, 30, 34, 37, 40)M.
2nd row – P, 24(27, 30, 34, 37, 40)M, work 2nd row of chart, p to end in M.
3rd to 27th rows – Rep the last 2 rows 12 times, then 1st row again but working rows 3 to 27 of Chart 1.
Continue in M only until work measures 29(33, 36, 37, 41, 43) cm / 11½(13, 14, 14½, 16, 17) in from beg, or desired length. Cast off *loosely*.

LEFT SLEEVE

Work as right sleeve, but working 24(36, 42, 42, 50, 58) rows in M in place of 6(8, 10, 12, 14, 16).

NECKBAND

First join shoulders. **With set of 3¼ mm needles and M**, right side facing, k across sts of back inc 7(4, 4, 3, 3, 3) sts evenly, k up 15(18, 18, 21, 24, 24) sts evenly down left front neck, k across centre sts inc 3(2, 2, 1, 1, 1) sts evenly, finally k up 15(18, 18, 21, 24, 24) sts evenly up right front neck.   *80(86, 90, 98, 108, 112) sts.*
Work 17 rounds of k1, p1 rib working in stripes of 1 row M, then 2 rows B, 2 rows C, 2 rows A, 10 rows M. Cast off *very loosely* in M.

TO MAKE UP

First embroider nose, whiskers and eye in black embroidery cotton on Peter. Omitting ribbing, press, following pressing instructions on ball band. Stitch cast-off edges of sleeves in position to yoke. Join side and sleeve seams. Fold neckband in half to wrong side and hem loosely in position. Press seams.

CHART 1

KEY

□ = M (Pink)

✗ = A (Brown)

• = B (Blue)

o = C (White)

Use a separate small ball of A, B and C for each colour area, and a separate ball of M at each side of Peter's body on rows 3 to 24.

17 pattern sts

Read odd rows k from right to left and even rows from left to right.

PUDDLE-DUCKS
DUNGAREES AND SWEATER

*– and the three Puddle-Ducks came along the hard high road, marching one
behind the other and doing the goose step – pit pat paddle pat! pit pat waddle pat!*

THE TALE OF TOM KITTEN

MEASUREMENTS

To fit chest	46–51	51–56	56–61	cm
	18–20	*20–22*	*22–24*	*in*

DUNGAREES

Length from top of bib	28	33	38	cm
to crotch, approx	*11*	*13*	*15*	*in*
Inner leg seam	24	29	34	cm
	9½	*11½*	*13½*	*in*

SWEATER

Length from shoulder	25	29	33	cm
	10	*11½*	*13*	*in*
Sleeve seam (adjustable)	18	21	25	cm
	7	*8½*	*10*	*in*

MATERIALS

Patons Cotton Supersoft, 50 g balls

DUNGAREES

Blue (B)	4	4	5

1 ball each Yellow (Y) and White (W).

SWEATER

Blue (B)	4	4	5

1 ball each Yellow (Y) and White (W).
A pair each 3¾ mm/No 9 and 3 mm/No 11 needles. 2
buttons for Dungarees. 4 buttons for Sweater. A length of
black embroidery thread.

TENSION

24 sts and 30 rows to 10 cm/4 in over st st on 3¾ mm/No 9
needles.

ABBREVIATIONS

K = knit; p = purl; sts = stitches; st st = stocking st; inc =
increase, increasing; dec = decrease, decreasing; beg =
beginning; alt = alternate; rep = repeat; tog = together; tbl =
through back of loops; cm = centimetres; in = inches; B =
Blue; Y = Yellow; W = White.

DUNGAREES

FRONT

Commence with right leg. **With 3 mm needles and B**, cast on
21(23, 25) sts loosely.

1st row (right side) – K2, [p1, k1] to last st, k1.
2nd row – K1, [p1, k1] to end.
Work 14(22, 30) more rows in rib.
Next row (hem) – Fold work in half and k to end, knitting
each st on needle tog with corresponding loop from cast-on
edge.
Next row – P4(4, 5), inc once in next 13(14, 15) sts, p to
end.   *34(37, 40) sts.*

Change to 3¾ mm needles and, beg with a k row, work
14(22, 30) rows in st st.
Carrying colours not in use loosely up side of work continue
in st st working [4 rows Y, 4 rows W, 4 rows B] 3 times, then 4
rows Y. Break Y and W. Continue in B for a few rows until
work measures 22(27, 32) cm/8¾(10¾, 12¾) in from beg,
ending after a k row.**

Shape leg by inc 1 st at *end* of next row and at same edge on
next 4 rows. Slip 39(42, 45) sts on a spare needle.

Work left leg as right leg to**.
Shape leg by inc 1 st at *beg* of next row and at same edge on
next 4 rows.   *39(42, 45) sts.*
Next row – K to end, cast on 5 sts, now with right side facing
k across sts on spare needle.   *83(89, 95) sts.*

Shape crotch thus:
1st and every alt row – P.
2nd row – K29(32, 35), k2 tog tbl, k21, k2 tog, k29(32, 35).
4th row – K29(32, 35), k2 tog tbl, k19, k2 tog, k to end.
6th row – K29(32, 25), k2 tog tbl, k17, k2 tog, k to end.
8th to 22nd rows – Continue in this way, dec 2 sts on every k
row.   *61(67, 73) sts.*
Work straight until front measures 10(13, 16) cm/4¼(5¼,
6¼) in from 5 cast-on sts, ending after a p row.

Continue in st st, **working from Chart 11** (see page 62) thus:
1st row – 1(3, 5)B, *work 1st row of chart, 1(2, 3)B; rep from *
once more, work 1st row of chart, 1(3, 5)B.
2nd to 20th rows – Rep 1st row 19 times but working rows 2
to 20 of Chart 11. Break Y and W. Continue in B and work 4
rows.

Shape bib thus:
1st row – K1, [k1, p1] 3 times, k to last 7 sts, [p1, k1] 3 times,
k1.

2nd row – K1, [p1, k1] 3 times, p to last 7 sts,[k1, p1] 3 times, k1.

Rep 1st and 2nd rows 0(2, 4) times more.

Next row – Rib 8, k2 tog tbl, k to last 10 sts, k2 tog, rib 8.

Next row – As 2nd.

Rep these 2 rows until 43(45, 47) sts remain. Work 1 row.***

Change to 3 mm needles and work 7 rows in rib on all sts as at commencement of legs.

Next row – K1, [p1, k1] 3 times, cast off centre 29(31, 33) sts evenly in rib, rib to end.

Continue in rib on last group of 7 sts for 10(13, 15) cm / 4(5, 6) in, or desired length. Cast off in rib.

With right side facing, rejoin B neatly to 7 sts. Complete as first strap.

BACK

Omitting Puddle-Ducks, work as front to ***, reading left leg for right leg, and right leg for left.

Change to 3 mm needles and work 2 rows in rib on all sts.

Next row – Rib 3, cast off 2 sts in rib, rib to last 5 sts, cast off 2 sts, rib to end.

Next row – In rib, casting on 2 sts in each place where sts were cast off.

Rib 3 more rows. Cast off in rib.

TO MAKE UP

Embroider an eye in black on each Puddle-Duck. Omitting ribbing, press, following pressing instructions on ball band.** Join side seams and inner leg seams. Sew buttons to straps. Press seams.

SWEATER

BUTTON BORDER

With 3¾ mm needles and B, cast on 21 sts. Work 6 rows in garter st. Slip sts on a spare needle.

FRONT AND BACK (worked sideways in one piece)

With 3 mm needles and B, cast on 31(33, 35) sts. Work 15(17, 19) rows in rib as on front of Dungarees.

Next row – Rib 8(6, 4), inc once in each of next 14(20, 26) sts, rib to end. *45(53, 61) sts.*

Change to 3¾ mm needles and, beg with a k row, work in st st until sleeve measures 9(13, 17) cm / 3½(5, 6½) in from beg, ending after a p row. (Length may be adjusted here.)

Continue in st st, **working from Chart 11** (see page 62) thus:

1st row – 13(17, 21)B, work 1st row of chart, 13(17, 21)B.

2nd to 20th rows – Rep 1st row 19 times but working rows 2 to 20 of chart. Break Y and W.

Continue in B and **shape sleeve** by inc 1 st at each end of next 6 rows. *57(65, 73) sts.*

Now cast on 18(21, 24) sts at beg of next 2 rows. *93(107, 121) sts.*

Work straight for 8(9, 10) cm / 3¼(3½, 4) in, ending after a p row.

Shape neck thus:

Next row – K41(47, 53), slip these sts on a length of yarn and leave, cast off next 6(7, 8) sts loosely, k to end.

Continue on last group of 46(53, 60) sts. Work 12(14, 14) rows straight.

Work **buttonhole band** thus:

1st row – P25(32, 39), k21.

2nd row – K.

3rd row – As 1st.

4th row – K3, [k2 tog, yarn forward, k4] 3 times, k to end.

5th and 6th rows – As 1st and 2nd.

7th row – P25(32, 39), cast off final 21 sts.

Next row – K across 21 button border sts, now with right side facing, k across 25(32, 39) sts. Work 11(13, 13) rows in st st on all sts, thus ending after a p row. Slip sts on a spare needle.

Slip front sts on length of yarn on to a 3¾ mm needle, point facing towards neck. Rejoin B. Dec 1 st at neck edge on next 3 rows. *38(44, 50) sts.*

Work 25(29, 29) rows straight. Inc 1 st at neck edge on next 3 rows. *41(47, 53) sts.*

Next row – K, cast on 6(7, 8) sts for second side of neck, now k across sts on spare needle. *93(107, 121) sts.*

Work straight for 8(9, 10) cm / 3¼(3½, 4) in, ending after a p row.

Shape sleeve by casting off 18(21, 24) sts loosely at beg of next 2 rows. Now dec 1 st at each end of next 6 rows. *45(53, 61) sts.*

Now reading *even* rows k from left to right and *odd* rows p from right to left, **work from Chart 11** thus:

1st row – 13(17, 21)B, work 20th row of Chart 11, reading from left to right, 13(17, 21)B.

2nd row – 13(17, 21)B, work 19th row from Chart 11, reading from right to left.

3rd to 20th rows – Continue in this way working chart rows in reverse order to correspond with Puddle-Duck on right sleeve. Break Y and W.

Continue in B until sleeve measures same as first sleeve to cuff, ending after a k row.

Next row – P8(6, 4), [p2 tog] 14(20, 26) times, p to end. *31(33, 35) sts.*

Change to 3 mm needles and rib 16(18, 20) rows. Cast off loosely in rib.

WELT

With 3 mm needles and B, right side facing, k up 61(67, 73) sts evenly along lower front edge. Beg with a 2nd row, work 18(20, 20) rows in rib as on front of Dungarees. Cast off loosely in rib. Work back welt the same.

NECKBAND

With 3 mm needles and B, right side facing, k up 11(13, 13) sts across left back, 37(42, 44) sts round front neck, finally 11(13, 13) sts from right back. *59(68, 70) sts.*

K 2 rows.

Next row – K1, k2 tog, yarn forward, k to end.

K 3 more rows. Cast off loosely.

TO MAKE UP

Make up as Dungarees to **. Join side and sleeve seams. Sew down lower edge of button border to wrong side. Sew on buttons. Press seams.

TOM KITTEN
CHILD'S SWEATER

Tom Kitten was very fat, and he had grown; several buttons burst off. His mother sewed them on again.

THE TALE OF TOM KITTEN

MEASUREMENTS

To fit chest					
	56	61	66	71	cm
	22	24	26	28	in
Length, approx	33	38	46	53	cm
	13	15	18	21	in
Nape of neck to wrist,	39	48	57	65	cm
approx	15½	19	22½	25½	in

MATERIALS

Richard Poppleton Plaza D K (M),

50 g balls	3	4	5	6

1 ball **Plaza D K** or **Poppletons Emmerdale D K** (50 g) each in 1st contrast (A) and 2nd contrast (B).
A pair each 4 mm / No 8 and 3¼ mm / No 10 needles. 3 small buttons.

TENSION

24 sts and 32 rows to 10 cm / 4 in over st st on 4 mm / No 8 needles.

ABBREVIATIONS

K = knit; p = purl; sts = stitches; st st = stocking st; inc = increase, increasing; dec = decrease, decreasing; foll = following; beg = beginning; alt = alternate; rep = repeat; cm = centimetres; in = inches.

FRONT

With 3¼ mm needles and A, cast on 67(73, 79, 85) sts.
1st row (right side) – K2, [p1, k1] to last st, k1.
2nd row – K1, [p1, k1] to end.
Work 14(18, 18, 22) more rows in rib, inc 8 sts evenly on last row. *75(81, 87, 93) sts.*

Break A. Join in M. **Change to 4 mm needles** and, beg with a k row, work 2(6, 18, 28) rows in st st. Carrying colour/s loosely over back of work, continue in st st, **working from Chart 8A** (see page 49) thus:
1st row – 8(11, 14, 17)M, work 1st row of chart, 8(11, 14, 17)M.
2nd to 10th rows – Rep 1st row 9 times but working rows 2 to 10 of Chart 8A. Break A.
Work 2(6, 10, 12) rows in M.

Using small balls of yarn for each colour area where possible,

otherwise carrying colour not in use *loosely* over not more than 5 sts at a time, and twisting yarns on wrong side when changing colour, continue in st st, **working from Chart 8B** (see page 49) thus:
1st row – 16(19, 22, 25)M, work 1st row of chart, 16(19, 22, 25)M.
2nd to 32nd rows – Rep 1st row 31 times but working rows 2 to 32 of Chart 8B.

Keeping chart correct, **shape sleeves** thus:
Inc 1 st at each end of next 4 rows. Now cast on 13(18, 23, 28) sts at beg of next 6 rows. *161(197, 233, 269) sts.*
N B. A third 4 mm needle may be used to hold the larger group of sts.

Work straight until 56th row of Chart 8B has been worked. Break A and B. Continue in M until work measures 6(7, 9, 10) cm / 2½(3, 3½, 4) in at *outer sleeve edge*, ending after a p row.

Shape neck thus:
Next row – K73(90, 107, 124), turn. Continue on this group. Dec 1 st at neck edge on next 4 rows. *69(86, 103, 120) sts.*
Work straight until front measures 10(11, 14, 15) cm / 4(4½, 5½, 6) in at *outer sleeve edge*, ending at sleeve edge.
Shape shoulder thus:
Cast off 45(59, 73, 87) sts loosely at beg of next row, and then 8(9, 10, 11) sts at beg of 2 foll alt rows. Work 1 row. Cast off.

With right side facing, slip centre 15(17, 19, 21) sts on a spare needle. Rejoin M and k 1 row. Complete as first side.

BACK

Omitting charts, work as front to neck shaping, ending after a p row.

Divide for neck opening thus:
Next row – K80(98, 116, 134), cast off centre st, k to end. Working 3 sts at inner edge in garter st continue on last group until back measures same as front to shoulder shaping, ending at sleeve edge.

Shape shoulder thus:
Cast off 45(59, 73, 87) sts loosely at beg of next row, then 8(9, 10, 11) sts at beg of 2 foll alt rows. Work 1 row. Cast off.

With wrong side facing, rejoin M and complete to match first side.

CHART 8B

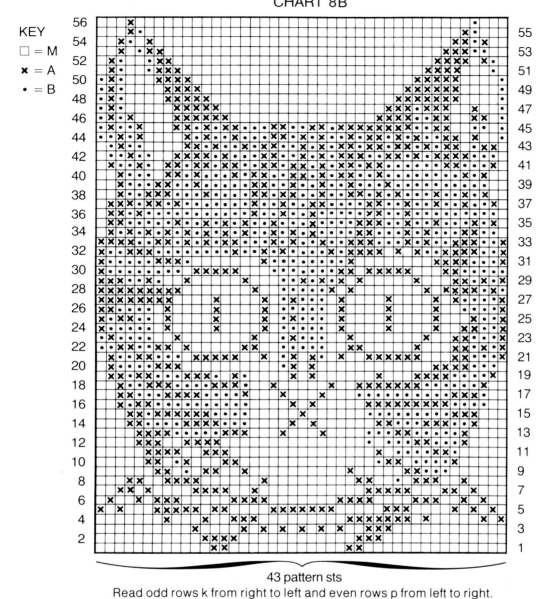

KEY
□ = M
✖ = A
• = B

43 pattern sts
Read odd rows k from right to left and even rows p from left to right.

CHART 8A

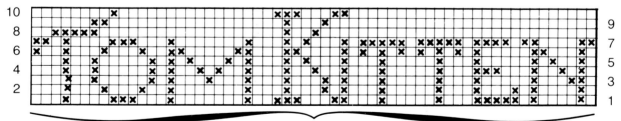

59 pattern sts

NECKBAND
First join shoulders. **With 3¼ mm needles and M**, right side facing, k up 59(65, 71, 77) sts evenly round neck including sts on spare needle. Beg with a 2nd row, work 6 rows in rib as on welt. Cast off evenly in rib.

CUFFS
With 3¼ mm needles and A, right side facing, k up 35(37, 41, 43) sts *firmly* along lower edge of sleeve. Beg with a 2nd row, work 16(20, 24, 24) rows in rib. Cast off loosely in rib.

TO MAKE UP
Omitting ribbing, press, following pressing instructions on ball band. Work 3 buttonhole loops evenly spaced in M on one back neck edge; sew on buttons to correspond on other edge. Join side and sleeve seams. Press seams.

MRS. TITTLEMOUSE
BABY TOP AND TROUSERS

And one day a little old woman ran up and down in a red spotty cloak.
'Your house is on fire, Mother Ladybird! Fly away home to your children!'
THE TALE OF MRS. TITTLEMOUSE

MEASUREMENTS

To fit chest	46	51	56	cm
	18	20	22	in

TOP
Length from shoulder	26	28	32	cm
	10¼	11¼	12½	in

TROUSERS
Inside leg seam	24	28	32	cm
	9½	11	12½	in
Front seam, excluding	17	18	20	cm
waist ribbing	6½	7¼	8	in

MATERIALS
Robin Landscape D K, 50 g balls
TOP
White (W)	2	2	2

An oddment of Black and Red (R)
TROUSERS
Red (R)	3	3	3

An oddment of Gold, White (W) and Black.
A pair each 4 mm/No 8 and 3¼ mm/No 10 needles. Shirring elastic for Trousers.

TENSION
22 sts and 30 rows to 10 cm/4 in over st st on 4 mm/No 8 needles.

ABBREVIATIONS
K = knit; p = purl; sts = stitches; st st = stocking st; m st = moss st; inc = increase, increasing; dec = decrease, decreasing; beg = beginning; foll = following; alt = alternate; rep = repeat; cm = centimetres; in = inches; W = White; R = Red.

TOP

FRONT AND BACK (2 pieces alike)
With 3¼ mm needles and W, cast on 45(51, 57) sts.
1st row (right side) – K2, [p1, k1] to last st, k1.
2nd row – K1, [p1, k1] to end.

Work 10 more rows in rib inc 7 sts evenly on last row. *52(58, 64) sts.*

Change to 4 mm needles.
Next row – K.
Next row – K1, p to last st, k1. Rep these 2 rows 11(13, 16) times more.

Using a separate ball of W for each side of Ladybird, and reading W for M on chart, **work from Chart 6** (see page 52) thus:
1st row – K, 18(21, 24)W, work 1st row of chart, 18(21, 24)W.
2nd row – K1W, p17(20, 23)W, work 2nd row of chart, p17(20, 23)W, k1W.
3rd and 4th rows – As 1st and 2nd, but working 3rd and 4th rows of Chart 6.
5th row (on which m st is introduced for armhole borders) – In W [k1, p1] 7(8, 9) times, k4(5, 6)W, work 5th row of chart, k4(5, 6)W, in W [p1, k1] to end.
6th row – In W [k1, p1] 7(8, 9) times, k1, p3(4, 5)W, work 6th row of chart, p3(4, 5)W, in W k1, [p1, k1] to end.
7th to 10th rows – Rep 5th and 6th rows twice but working 7th to 10th rows of chart.
Keeping chart and m st correct, **shape square armholes** thus: In W cast off 9(11, 13) sts in m st at beg of next 2 rows. *34(36, 38) sts.*
Keeping chart and 6 sts at each end of rows in m st correct, work 3 rows, thus completing chart. Continue in W only for 9(11, 13) rows, dec 1 st at centre of last row. *33(35, 37) sts.*
Next 7 rows – P1, [k1, p1] to end.

Shape square neck thus:
Next row (wrong side) – m st 7(7, 8), cast off centre 19(21, 21) sts in m st, m st to end.
Continue on last group of 7(7, 8) sts until work measures 11(13, 14) cm/4½(5, 5½) in from armhole cast-off. Cast off in m st. With right side facing, rejoin W neatly to remaining sts and complete as first side.

TO MAKE UP
First embroider legs and feelers in black. Omitting ribbing, press following pressing instructions on ball band.** Join side seams and shoulders. Press seams.

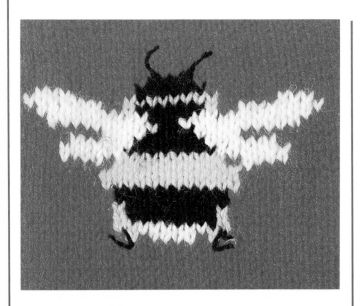

TROUSERS

RIGHT LEG

With 3¼ mm needles and R, cast on 39(41, 43) sts. Work 15 rows in rib as on Top.
Next row – Rib 5(3, 1), [inc in next st, rib 2] 9(11, 13) times, inc in next st, rib to end.   *49(53, 57) sts.*

Change to 4 mm needles and, beg with a k row, work in st st, shaping leg by inc 1 st at each end of 3rd(7th, 11th) row, then on every foll 8th row until there are 57(63, 69) sts. Work 3 rows. Shaping is now complete.

Continue in st st and using a separate ball of R for each side of Bee, and reading R for M, **work from Chart 7** thus:
1st row – K, 7(10, 13)R, work 1st row of chart, 24(27, 30)R.

2nd row – P, 24(27, 30)R, work 2nd row of chart, 7(10, 13)R.
3rd to 19th rows – Rep 1st and 2nd rows 8 times, then 1st row again, but working 3rd to 19th rows of chart.
Continue in R only and p 1 row.
Now inc 1 st at each end of every row until there are 73(79, 85) sts. Place a marker at centre of last row.
Work 2 rows straight. Now dec 1 st at each end of every k row until 63(69, 75) sts remain, then on every foll 6th row until 53(59, 63) sts remain.
Continue straight until leg measures 17(18, 20) cm/6½(7¼, 8) in from marker, ending after a k row.**

Shape back thus:
1st row – P30, turn.
2nd and alt rows – Slip 1, k to end.
3rd row – P25, turn.
5th row – P20, turn.
7th row – P15, turn.
9th row – P10, turn.
10th row – Slip 1, k to end.
11th row – P to end, dec 6 sts evenly.   *47(53, 57) sts.*

Change to 3¼ mm needles and, beg with a 1st row, work 7 rows in rib as on Top. Cast off loosely in rib.

LEFT LEG
Omitting Bee, work as right leg to ** but ending after a p row.

Shape back and complete as for right leg but reading k for p and p for k on shaping rows, and commencing with a 2nd rib row for waist.

TO MAKE UP
Make up as Top to **. Join front and back seams and inner leg seams. Run 3–4 rows of shirring elastic through wrong side of waist ribbing, drawing up slightly to fit waist and securing ends firmly. Press seams.

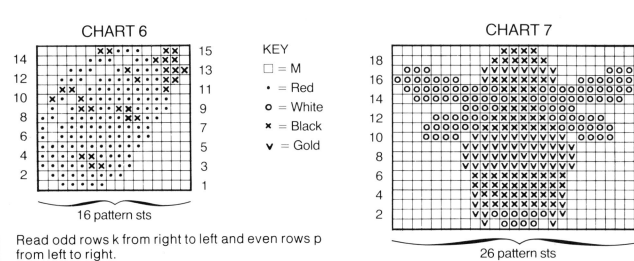

CHART 6

14 15
12 13
10 11
8   9
6   7
4   5
2   3
    1

16 pattern sts

Read odd rows k from right to left and even rows p from left to right.

KEY
□ = M
• = Red
o = White
× = Black
v = Gold

CHART 7

18 19
16 17
14 15
12 13
10 11
8   9
6   7
4   5
2   3
    1

26 pattern sts

Use small balls of yarn for each colour area where possible, twisting yarns on wrong side when changing colour.

FLOPSY BUNNIES
BABY'S JUMPER

Mr. McGregor threw down the sack on the stone floor in a way that would have been extremely painful to the Flopsy Bunnies, if they had happened to have been inside it.

THE TALE OF THE FLOPSY BUNNIES

MEASUREMENTS

To fit chest	46	51	56	61	cm
	18	*20*	*22*	*24*	*in*
Length at centre	27	29	33	36	cm
back, excluding	*10½*	*11¾*	*13*	*14¼*	*in*
neckband, approx					
Sleeve seam	15	18	21	24	cm
	6	*7*	*8¼*	*9½*	*in*

MATERIALS

Robin Bambino Raindrop DK (M), 40 g balls

	3	3	4	4

1 ball of **Robin Landscape DK** in Light Brown and an oddment of White mohair or double knitting. A pair each 4mm/No 8 and 3¼ mm/No 10 needles. 3 small buttons. Few lengths of dark brown embroidery thread. Oddments of ribbon.

TENSION

22 sts and 30 rows to 10 cm/4 in over st st on 4 mm/No 8 needles.

ABBREVIATIONS

K = knit; p = purl; sts = stitches; st st = stocking st; g st = garter st; inc = increase, increasing; dec = decrease, decreasing; tog = together; tbl = through back of loops; yfwd = yarn forward; rep = repeat; cm = centimetres; in = inches.

FRONT

With 3¼ mm needles and M, cast on 49(55, 61, 67) sts.
1st row – K2, [p1, k1] to last st, k1.
2nd row – K1, [p1, k1] to end.
Work 8(10, 12, 14) more rows in rib, inc 5 sts evenly on last row. *54(60, 66, 72) sts.*

Change to 4 mm needles and, beg with a k row, work 4(6, 6, 8) rows in st st.
Using small balls of yarn for each colour area where possible, twisting yarns on wrong side when changing colour, continue in st st, **working from Chart 9** (see page 55) thus:
1st row – 2(5, 8, 11)M, work 1st row of chart, 2(5, 8, 11)M.

2nd to 31st rows – Rep 1st row 30 times but working rows 2 to 31 of Chart 9.
Continue in M only and work 3(5, 7, 9) rows.

Shape raglan thus:
1st and 2nd rows – Cast off 2 sts, work to end.
3rd row – K1, k2 tog tbl, k to last 3 sts, k2 tog, k1.
4th row – K1, p2 tog, p to last 3 sts, p2 tog tbl, k1.

3rd and 4th sizes only
Rep 3rd and 4th rows once.

All sizes
Next row – As 3rd.
Next row – K1, p to last st, k1.
Rep the last 2 rows until 28(32, 32, 36) sts remain, ending after a p row.

Shape neck thus:
Next row – K1, k2 tog tbl, k 7(8, 8, 9), turn.
Continue on this group. Still dec at raglan edge as before, *at the same time* dec 1 st at neck edge on next 3 rows. *5(6, 6, 7) sts.*
Continue dec at raglan edge only until 2 sts remain. Work 1 row. Fasten off.

With right side facing, slip centre 8(10, 10, 12) sts on a spare needle. Rejoin M and k to last 3 sts, k2 tog, k1. Complete as first side.

BACK

Omitting motif, work as front until 40(42, 42, 44) sts remain in the raglan shaping, ending after a p row.

Divide for neck opening thus:
Next row – K1, k2 tog tbl, k19(20, 20, 21), turn.
Continue on this group. Working 4 sts at inner edge in g st, work 5 rows still dec as before.

Next row (buttonhole row) – K1, k2 tog tbl, k to last 3 sts, yfwd, k2 tog, k1.
Working 4 sts at inner edge in g st, work 9 rows still dec as before.

Work buttonhole row again. Work 5 more rows still dec as before. Slip final 11(12, 12, 13) sts on to a spare needle.

With M, cast on 4 sts for button flap on to empty 4 mm needle. Using this needle, with right side facing, k to last 3 sts, k2 tog, k1.
Working 4 sts at inner edge in g st, continue dec at raglan edge on every k row as before until 11(12, 12, 13) sts remain. Work 1 row. Slip sts on to a spare needle.

SLEEVES

With 3¼ mm needles and M, cast on 27(29, 31, 33) sts. Work 10(12, 14, 16) rows in rib as on welt, inc 5 sts evenly on last row.   *32(34, 36, 38) sts.*

Change to 4 mm needles and, beg with a k row, work in st st, shaping sleeve by inc 1 st at each end of 1st row, then on every following 6th row until there are 44(48, 52, 56) sts. Work a few rows straight until sleeve measures 15(18, 21, 24) cm / 6(7, 8¼, 9½) in, ending after a p row.

Shape raglan thus:
1st to 4th rows – As on front.
Rep 3rd and 4th rows once more.
Next row – As 3rd.
Next row – K1, p to last st, k1.
Rep the last 2 rows until 6 sts remain, ending after a p row.
Slip sts on to a spare needle.

NECKBAND

First join raglan shapings. **With 3¼ mm needles and M**, right side facing, k across sts of left back, then left sleeve, k up 25(31, 31, 35) sts evenly round front neck including sts on

spare needle, finally k across sts of right sleeve and right back.   *59(67, 67, 73) sts.*
1st row – K4, [p1, k1] to last 3 sts, k3.
2nd row – K5, [p1, k1] to last 4 sts, k4.
3rd row – As 1st.
4th row – Work to last 3 sts, yfwd, k2 tog, k1.
5th and 6th rows – As 1st and 2nd. Cast off evenly.

TO MAKE UP

First embroider eyes, nose and whiskers in dark brown on each rabbit. Omitting ribbing, press, following pressing instructions on Rainbow D K ball band. Join side and sleeve seams. Sew down button flap on wrong side. Sew on buttons. Using a bodkin, slot ribbon round necks of rabbits and tie in a small bow. Catch ribbon at points where it is slotted through knitting and secure bows. Press seams.

CHART 9

KEY

□ = M

• = Brown

✕ = White mohair or double knitting

Read odd rows k from right to left and even rows p from left to right.

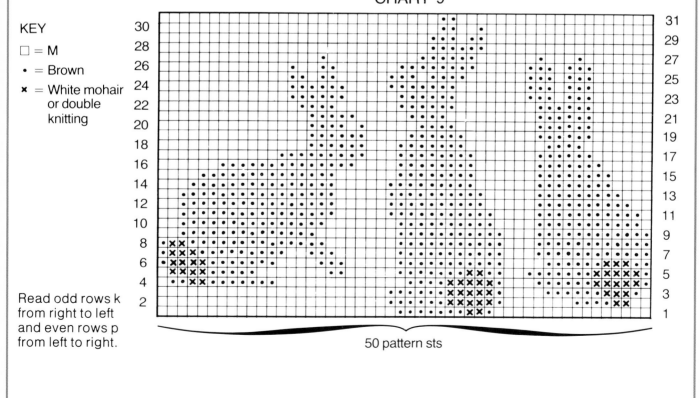

50 pattern sts

MRS. TITTLEMOUSE
COT BLANKET

*There was a kitchen, a parlour, a pantry, and a larder. Also, there was
Mrs. Tittlemouse's bedroom, where she slept in a little box bed!*
THE TALE OF MRS. TITTLEMOUSE

MEASUREMENTS
Approx 91 cm/36 in × 132 cm/52 in.

MATERIALS
Hayfield Brushed Chunky,   6 balls (100 g) in White (M),
1 ball in Pink (A) and 1 ball in Blue (B).
A pair each 5½ mm/No 5 and 7 mm/No 2 needles.

TENSION
14 sts and 19 rows to 10 cm/4 in over patt section on
7 mm/No 2 needles.

ABBREVIATIONS
K = knit; p = purl; sts = stitches; patt = pattern; g st = garter
st; st st = stocking st; inc = increase, increasing; sl = slip;
yfwd = yarn forward; tog = together; rep = repeat; cm =
centimetres; in = inches.

TO MAKE
With 5½ mm needles and M, cast on 127 sts. Work 8 rows in
g st.
Next row (wrong side) – K6, and slip these 6 sts on to a
safety-pin, *inc purlways in next st, p21, inc purlways in
next st, slip the last 25 sts on a length of yarn and leave*,
work from * to * 4 times more, k6.
Continue in g st on these 6 sts for left border until strip
measures 122 cm/48 in from cast-on edge, ending after a
right-side row. Slip sts on a safety-pin and leave.

With right side facing, slip first group of 25 sts on to a 7 mm
needle (i.e. group next to g st strip just worked). Continue
on 7 mm needles and, joining in and breaking off colours as
required, work **first strip** in patt thus:
1st row In A, k1, p1, [with yarn front sl1 purlways, p1] to last
st, k1.
2nd row – In A, p.
3rd row – In M, k2, [yfwd, k2 tog] to last st, k1.
4th row – In M, p.
5th and 6th rows – As 1st and 2nd.
7th row – In M, k2, [k2 tog, yfwd] to last st, k1.

8th row – In M, p.
9th to 12th rows – As 1st to 4th.
13th row – As 1st.
14th to 24th rows – In M, beg with a p row, work 11 rows in st
st.
Rep the last 24 rows 8 times more, then rows 1 to 12 again.
Next row – In M, k2 tog, k21, k2 tog. Slip 23 sts on a length of
yarn.

**With right side facing, slip next group of 25 sts on to a
7 mm needle. Continue on 7 mm needles and work **second
strip** thus:
1st to 10th rows – In M, beginning with a k row, work 10
rows in st st.
11th to 23rd rows – Using B in place of A, as rows 1 to 13 of
first strip.
24th row – In M, p.
Rep the last 24 rows 8 times more, then rows 1 to 10 again.
Next row – In M, k2 tog, k21, k2 tog. Slip 23 sts on a length of
yarn.**

With right side facing, slip next group of 25 sts on to a 7 mm
needle and work as first strip.

Now work from ** to **.

With right side facing, slip final group of 25 sts on to a 7 mm
needle and work as first strip.

With right side facing, slip next 6 sts at lower edge on to a 5½
mm needle. Rejoin M and continue in g st until right border
measures same as left border, ending after a wrong-side
row.
Now commencing with 6 sts of left border on safety-pin, slip
the 6 groups of sts on to the empty 5½ mm needle and, using
the needle holding 6 right border sts, p115, k6 across sts on
left needle.   *127 sts.*
Work 7 rows in g st. Cast off loosely knitways.

TO COMPLETE
Do not press. Join 4 inner seams using a back-stitch seam.
Overlapping g st border over edge of main part, sew borders
in position.

57

FLOPSY BUNNIES
TUFTED RUG

'One, two, three, four, five, six leetle fat rabbits!' repeated Mr. McGregor,
counting on his fingers – 'one, two, three –'
THE TALE OF THE FLOPSY BUNNIES

MEASUREMENTS
Finished rug size: 69 × 129 cm / 27 × 51 in.

MATERIALS
Patons Turkey Rug Wool (360 pieces per cut pack)
Shade   975   30 packs
         973   6 packs
         940   4 packs
         900 and 501 2 packs each
         941, 903, 960, 930, 877, 894 and 983, 1 pack each
N B. To ensure all shades are the same dye lot, it is advisable
to purchase large amounts together.
3 balls **Patons Turkey Binding Wool**, shade 975 (optional).
Patons Brown check canvas 69 × 137 cm / 27 × 54 in.
1 Patons latchet hook.

RUG-MAKING AT HOME
Rug-making is most simple if you sit at a table with one end
of the canvas facing you, so that the knots are worked on the
line of canvas which lies on the edge of the table; a weight
placed on the unworked canvas will assist in supporting the
worked part of the rug.

MAKING THE KNOT
The knots can be made by either Method 1 or Method 2.
They are equally quick and the only difference is that the pile
fabrics worked by the two methods lie in different direc-
tions. This can be turned to advantage so as to enable two

people to work at the rug from opposite ends of the canvas
towards the middle. If one person uses Method 1 and the
other Method 2 all the complete pile will lie in the same
direction.

TO MAKE
Fold under 4 cm / 1½ in of the canvas across the width of the
starting edge and work through the canvas: this gives a neat,
strong finish.
     Always work in rows across the width of the canvas
from selvedge to selvedge. Knot through every stitch following Chart 10 on pages 60 and 61. Do not work blocks of
pattern or colours separately.
     The last few rows are worked double in the same way as
the starting edge.

BINDING THE SELVEDGES (optional)
Using shade 975 work as for Stitched Rug on page 114.
     To give the rug a smooth, even surface, clip any long ends
with sharp scissors; this will give the rug a professional
finish but care must be taken. Remove loose ends with
Sellotape or a damp cloth.

RUG CARE AND CLEANING
Shake out loose dirt and vacuum clean both sides of the rug.
With a cloth or brush moistened in liquid detergent lightly
clean the pile. If required, light hand-shampooing machines
may be used. Dry by hanging the rug on a line away from

Method 1

1 Fold one piece of wool exactly in half round the shank of the hook; the eveness of the pile depends on this precise fold.

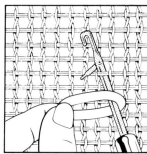

2 Push the hook under the strands of canvas (weft) where the knot is to be made.

3 Push the hook forward and ensure the latch is free to open, and turn the hook slightly to the right.

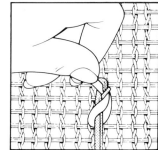

4 Pull the hook through the loop of wool and push hook forward. Gently pull the two ends of the wool to make the knot firm.

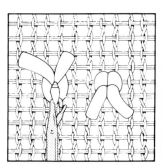

59

direct sunlight or by laying it flat. The rug may be drycleaned professionally if desired.

Do not attach any backing material such as hessian, etc.

Do not use a washing machine or allow the rug to become soaking wet. Do not use heavy electrical or commercial shampooing machines or tumble dry.

Method 2

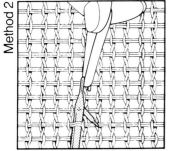

1 Push the hook under the strand of canvas (weft) where the knot is to be made until the latch lies behind the canvas. Fold one piece of wool in half and place this in the hook, ensuring the two ends are exactly the same length.

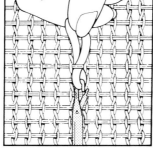

2 Pull the hook back towards you so that about a third of the wool is in front and two thirds behind the canvas weft threads.

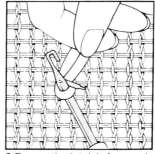

3 Ensure the latch is free and open and place the free ends of the wool through the hook. Then allow the latch to close over the wool.

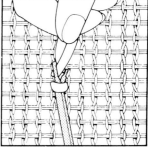

4 Place the free ends of the wool through the hook and let the latch close.

5 Pull the hook backwards and gently pull the knot to make it firm.

CHART 10

60

□ 975 Background △ 960 s 877 ✖ 894 ✎ 900 v 941 z 983 ■ 903 ୪ 930 ↑ 940

•501　　o973

Jemima Puddle-Duck
PRAM RUG

She laid some more in June, and she was permitted to keep them herself: but only four of them hatched. Jemima Puddle-Duck said that it was because of her nerves; but she had always been a bad sitter.

THE TALE OF JEMIMA PUDDLE-DUCK

MEASUREMENTS

Approx 66 cm/26 in × 91 cm/36 in

MATERIALS

Twilleys Capricorn Bulky, 4 balls (100g) in Blue, 1 ball each Yellow and White.
A pair 6 mm/No 4 needles. A length of black embroidery thread.

TENSION

14 sts and 19 rows to 10 cm/4 in over stocking st.

ABBREVIATIONS

K = knit; p = purl; sts = stitches; g st = garter st; inc = increase, increasing; tog = together; beg = beginning; rep = repeat; B = Blue; Y = Yellow; W = White.

TO MAKE

With B, cast on 80 sts. Work 8 rows in g st.
Next row – K6, p1, [inc purlways in next st, p7] 8 times, inc in next st, p2, k6. *89 sts.*
Next row (right side) – K.
Next row – K6, p77, k6.
Rep the last 2 rows until work measures 24 cm/9½ in from beg, ending after a wrong-side row.

Work Puddle-Ducks from Chart 11 thus:
1st row – K, 21B, work 1st row of chart, 49B.
2nd row – K6B, p43B, work 2nd row of chart, p15B, k6B.
3rd to 20th rows – Rep 1st and 2nd rows 9 times but working rows 3 to 20 of Chart 11.
21st to 26th rows – Work 6 rows all in B as before.
27th row – K, 35B, work 1st row of chart, 35B.
28th row – K6B, p29B, work 2nd row of chart, p29B, k6B.
29th to 46th rows – Rep 27th and 28th rows 9 times but working rows 3 to 20 of Chart 11.
47th to 52nd rows – Work 6 rows all in B as before.
53rd row – K, 49B, work 1st row of chart, 21B.
54th row – K6B, p15B, work 2nd row of chart, p43B, k6B.

55th to 72nd rows – Rep 53rd and 54th rows 9 times, but working rows 3 to 20 of Chart 11.
Continue in B only as before until work measures 76 cm/30 in from beg, ending after a k row.
Next row – K6, p1, [p2 tog, p7] 8 times, p2 tog, p2, k6. *80 sts.*
Change to g st and work straight until rug measures 91 cm/36 in, ending after a wrong-side row. Cast off *loosely*.

Do not press. Embroider an eye in black on each Puddle-Duck.

CHART 11

KEY

□ = B (Blue)
✕ = Y (Yellow)
• = W (White)

Read odd rows k from right to left and even rows p from left to right.

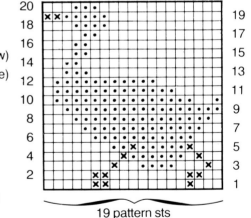

19 pattern sts

Use a separate small ball of y for each y area, and a separate ball of B on row 3 to 12 at each side of duck's body. Twist yarns on wrong side when changing colour.

62

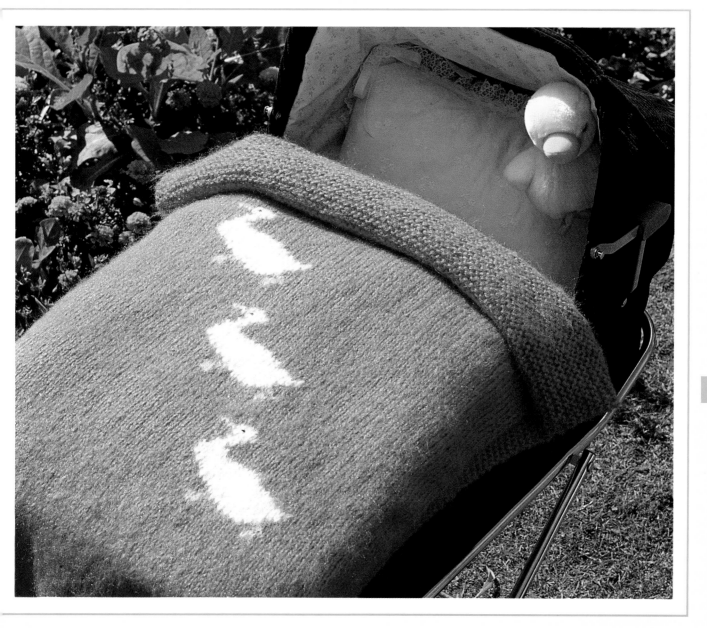

BENJAMIN BUNNY
SWEATER, PULL-UPS AND TAM-O'-SHANTER

Benjamin tried on the tam-o'-shanter, but it was too big for him.

THE TALE OF BENJAMIN BUNNY

MEASUREMENTS

SWEATER

To fit chest	46	51	56	61	cm
	18	*20*	*22*	*24*	*in*
Length from shoulder,	26	30	34	38	cm
approx	*10¼*	*12*	*13½*	*15*	*in*
Nape of neck to wrist,	29	34	41	47	cm
approx	*11½*	*13½*	*16*	*18½*	*in*

PULL-UPS

Inside leg	24	28	32	36	cm
	9½	*11*	*12½*	*14*	*in*
Front waist to crotch,	17	18	20	22	cm
excluding ribbing	*6½*	*7¼*	*8*	*8¾*	*in*

TAM-O-SHANTER
To fit an average baby/toddler

MATERIALS

Wendy Family Choice D K, 50 g balls

SWEATER

Main shade (M – White)	2	3	3	3

1 ball (50 g) in Red; an oddment each in Brown, Fawn, Tan and Green; also a small oddment in White if White has not been chosen for main shade.

PULL-UPS

Main shade (M – White)	1	1	2	2

1 ball (50 g) each Green, Brown and Red.

TAM-O-SHANTER
2 balls (50 g) in Green; an oddment in Red.
A pair each 4 mm/No 8 and 3¼ mm/No 10 needles. 3 buttons for Sweater; few lengths of shirring elastic for Pull-ups. 1 skein Anchor stranded cotton in dark brown.

TENSION
24 sts and 32 rows to 10 cm/4 in over st st on 4 mm/No 8 needles.

ABBREVIATIONS
K = knit; p = purl; sts = stitches; st st = stocking st; g st = garter st; inc = increase, increasing; dec = decrease, decreasing; tog = together; beg = beginning; foll = following; rep = repeat; cm = centimetres; in = inches; M = main shade; B = Brown; F = Fawn; R = Red; T = Tan; G = Green; W = White.

SWEATER

FRONT

With 3¼ mm needles and R, cast on 55(61, 67, 73) sts.
1st row (right side) – K2, [p1, k1] to last st, k1.
2nd row – K1, [p1, k1] to end.
Work 10(12, 16, 16) more rows in rib, inc 9 sts evenly on last row. *64(70, 76, 82) sts.* Break R.

Change to 4 mm needles and M and, beg with a k row, work 2(14, 20, 30) rows in st st.
Continue in st st, **working from Chart 12** thus (N B. If White is used for main shade, the symbol for White on the chart should be ignored):
1st row – 18(21, 24, 27)M, work 1st row of chart, 18(21, 24, 27)M. Continue with chart as placed on last row until 34th (30th, 28th, 26th) row of Chart 12 has been worked.

Keeping chart correct and working extra sts into M, **shape sleeves** thus:
Inc 1 st at each end of next 6 rows. Cast on 22(31, 40, 52) sts at beg of next 2 rows. *120(144, 168, 198) sts.***
Work straight until 52nd row of chart has been worked. Continue in M and work 6 rows.

Shape neck thus:
Next row – K53(64, 75, 89), turn.
Continue on this group. Dec 1 st at neck edge on next 3 rows. *50(61, 72, 86) sts.*
Work 4(4, 6, 8) rows straight. ***Break M. Join in R.

Change to 3¼ mm needles and work 7 rows in g st. Cast off *loosely.***

With right side facing, slip centre 14(16, 18, 20) sts on a spare needle. Rejoin M and k 1 row. Complete as first side.

CHART 12

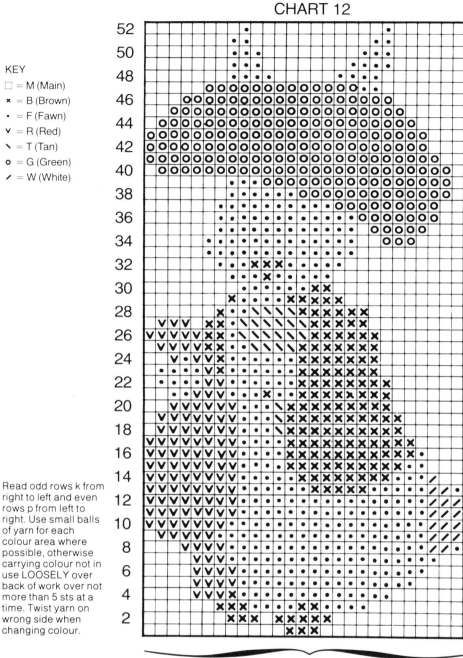

28 pattern sts

Read odd rows k from right to left and even rows p from left to right. Use small balls of yarn for each colour area where possible, otherwise carrying colour not in use LOOSELY over back of work over not more than 5 sts at a time. Twist yarn on wrong side when changing colour.

BACK

Omitting chart, work as front to **. Work 24(28, 32, 36) rows straight. Work as front from *** to ***.

FRONT NECKBAND

With 3¼ mm needles and R, right side facing, k up 34(36, 42, 48) sts evenly round front neck including sts on spare needle. Work 6 rows in g st. Cast off loosely.

CUFFS

Commencing at sleeve edge, first join left shoulder, including neckband, matching st for st. Join right shoulder in same way but leave final 7 cm/3 in free at neck edge on right shoulder. **With 3¼ mm needles and R**, right side facing, k up 31(33, 35, 37) sts evenly and firmly along one sleeve edge.

Beg with a 2nd row, work 14(14, 18, 18) rows in rib as on front. Cast off *loosely* in rib.

TO MAKE UP

First embroider Benjamin's eyes and nose with brown stranded cotton, then using a split length outline sleeve and the paw holding the onion. Using a single strand of the cotton, embroider whiskers. Using G, embroider onion leaves. Using a short, split length of W, embroider spots and stripes on handkerchief.** Omitting ribbing, press, following pressing instructions on ball band. Join side and sleeve seams. Make a small pompon in R and attach to top of tam-o-shanter. Work 3 buttonhole loops on front, right shoulder; sew on buttons to correspond on back shoulder. Press seams.

65

PULL-UPS

RIGHT HALF

Begin at crotch. **With 4 mm needles and G**, cast on 3 sts and p 1 row.

1st row – K to last st, inc in last st.
2nd row – Inc in first st, p to end.
3rd to 6th rows – Rep 1st and 2nd rows twice. *9 sts.*
7th row – Inc in first st, k to end, cast on 3 sts.
8th row – P to last st, inc in last st.
9th row – Inc in first st, k to end, cast on 5 sts.
10th row – As 8th. *21 sts.*
11th row – Cast on 41(50, 56, 62) sts, k to end, cast on 7 sts.
12th row – P.
13th row – K to end, cast on 9 sts.
14th row – P.
15th row – K to end, cast on 14(19, 23, 27) sts. *92(106, 116, 126) sts.*
Purl 1 row, thus ending at lower edge. Mark centre of last row.

Joining in and breaking off R, B and G, continue in st st working in stripes of 2 rows W, 2 rows R, 2 rows W, 2 rows B, 2 rows W, 2 rows G repeated throughout, and *at the same time* shape back by dec 1 st at top edge on 5th row foll, then on every foll 6th row until 84(98, 108, 118) sts remain.
Continue straight until work measures 27(29, 32, 34) cm/ 10½(11½, 12½, 13½) in from marker, ending after a p row in W. Break W, R and B. Continue in G and k 1 row.

Shape second half thus:
1st row – Cast off 6(11, 15, 19) sts, p to end.
2nd row – Cast off 38(47, 53, 59) sts, k to end.
3rd row – Cast off 9 sts, p to last 2 sts, p2 tog.
4th row – K2 tog, k to end.
5th row – Cast off 7 sts, p to last 2 sts, p2 tog.
6th row – As 4th.
7th row – Cast off 5 sts, p to last 2 sts, p2 tog.
8th row – As 4th.
9th row – Cast off 3 sts, p to last 2 sts, p2 tog. *9 sts.*
10th row – K to last 2 sts, k2 tog.
11th row – P2 tog, p to end.
Rep 10th and 11th rows until 3 sts remain. Work 1 row. Cast off.

LEFT HALF

Reading k for p, and p for k, work as first half.

LEG RIBBING

With 3¼ mm needles and R, right side facing, k up 35(39, 43, 47) sts evenly and firmly along lower leg edge. Beg with a 2nd row, work 18(18, 22, 26) rows in rib as on front of Sweater. Cast off *loosely* in rib.

WAIST RIBBING

First join centre-front seam. **With 3¼ mm needles and R**, right side facing, k up 107(119, 131, 143) sts *evenly* along top edge. Beg with a 2nd row, work 8 rows in rib as on front of Sweater. Cast off *loosely* in rib.

TO MAKE UP

Press as Sweater. Join centre-back seam and inner leg seams.

Run 4–5 rows of shirring elastic along inner edge of waist ribbing, drawing up to fit waist and securing ends firmly. Press seams.

TAM-O'-SHANTER

With 3¼ mm needles and G, cast on 95 sts. Work 10 rows in rib as on front of Sweater, inc 6 sts evenly on last row. *101 sts.*

Change to 4 mm needles and work thus:

1st row – [K9, inc in next st] 10 times, k1.
2nd row – P.
3rd row – [K10, inc in next st] 10 times, k1.
4th row – K (thus forming a ridge).
5th row – [K11, inc in next st] 10 times, k1.
6th row – P.
7th row – [K12, inc in next st] 10 times, k1.
8th row – K.
Continue in this way, inc 10 sts on every k row and working a ridge row on every foll 4th row until there are 181 sts. Continue in ridged st st until work measures 15 cm / 6 in from centre of ribbing, ending after a p row.

Shape crown thus:
1st row – [K18, k2 tog] 9 times, k1.
2nd row – K.
3rd row – [K17, k2 tog] 9 times, k1.
4th row – P.
5th row – [K16, k2 tog] 9 times, k1.
Continue in this way dec 9 sts evenly on every right-side row until 37 sts remain. Break yarn. Thread end through sts, draw up and fasten off. Join seam. Fold ribbing in half to wrong side and hem in position. Using R, make a pompon and attach to top of crown.

BENJAMIN BUNNY
SLEEPING BAG

Little Benjamin said that the first thing to be done was to get back Peter's
clothes, in order that they might be able to use the pocket-handkerchief.
They took them off the scarecrow.

THE TALE OF BENJAMIN BUNNY

MEASUREMENTS
Width all round at underarms approx 76 cm/30 in
Length 66 cm/26 in

MATERIALS
Wendy Peter Pan Darling DK, 6 balls (40 g) in main colour (M).
1 ball (40 g) or oddment of **Wendy Family Choice DK** in Brown, Fawn, Red, Tan, Green and White. A pair each 4 mm/No 8 and 3¼ mm/No 10 needles. A 51 cm/20 in zip-fastener. 1 button. Few lengths of Anchor stranded cotton in dark brown.

TENSION
24 sts and 32 rows to 10 cm/4 in over st st on 4 mm/No 8 needles.

ABBREVIATIONS
K = knit; p = purl; sts = stitches; st st = stocking st; g st = garter st; inc = increase; dec = decrease; beg = beginning; alt = alternate; foll = following; rep = repeat; cm = centimetres; in = inches.

FRONT
With 4 mm needles and M, cast on 90 sts. Beg with a k row, work in st st for 10 cm/4¼ in, ending after a p row.

Divide for zip thus:
Next row – K45 and slip these sts on a length of yarn and leave, k to end. Continue on last group.
Next row – P42, k1, p1, k1.

Work from Chart 12 (see page 65) thus:
1st row – K4M, work 1st row of chart, k13M.
2nd row – P13M, work 2nd row of chart, in M [p1, k1] twice.
3rd to 52nd rows – Rep 1st and 2nd rows 25 times but working rows 3 to 52 of Chart 12.
Continue in M only until work measures 52 cm/20¾ in from beg, ending after a wrong-side row.

Shape sleeve thus:
Inc 1 st at side edge on next 5 rows.
Now cast on 3 sts at beg of next row, then on every foll alt row until there are 68 sts.
Work 10 rows straight, thus ending at neck edge.

Shape neck thus:
Cast off 7 sts at beg of next row. Dec 1 st at neck edge on next 5 rows. *56 sts.*
Work 9 rows straight. Cast off.

With wrong side facing, slip sts on length of yarn on to a 4 mm needle. Rejoin M neatly.
Next row – K1, p1, k1, p to end.
Next row – K.
Rep these 2 rows until work measures 36 rows less than right half up to sleeve shaping, thus ending after a wrong-side row.

Work from Chart 12 thus:
1st row – K13M, work 1st row of chart, k4M.
2nd row – In M, [k1, p1] twice, work 2nd row of chart, p13M.
3rd to 35th rows – Rep 1st and 2nd rows 16 times, then 1st row again but working rows 3 to 35 of chart.

Keeping chart correct, **shape sleeve** as on right half. Work 1 row straight, thus completing chart. Continue in M. Work 9 rows straight. Shape neck and complete as right half.

BACK
With 4 mm needles and M, cast on 90 sts. Beg with a k row, work in st st until back measures same as fronts to sleeve shaping, ending after a k row.

Shape sleeves thus:
Inc 1 st at each end of next 5 rows. Cast on 3 sts at beg of every row until there are 136 sts. Work 24 rows straight.
Next row – Cast off 56 sts, k24 (including st on needle after cast-off), slip these 24 sts on a spare needle, cast off remaining 56 sts.

BUTTONHOLE TAB AND NECKBAND

First join shoulders. **With 3¼ mm needles and M**, cast on 8 sts. Work 4 rows in g st.

Next row – K3, cast off 2 sts, k to end. Using needle holding these sts and with right side facing, k up 19 sts evenly round right front neck, k across 24 sts of back, finally k up 19 sts round left front neck.   *68 sts.*

Next row – K, casting on 2 sts over those cast off. Work 3 rows g st. Cast off evenly.

CUFFS

With 3¼ mm needles and M, right side facing, k up 36 sts evenly and firmly from one sleeve edge. Work 12 rows in g st. Cast off loosely.

TO MAKE UP

Make up as Sweater to ** (see page 65). Press, following pressing instructions on ball band. Join side and sleeve seams and lower edge. Leaving neckband and buttonhole tab free, sew in zip. Stitch inner edge of first 4 rows of buttonhole tab to right front edge. Sew on button to correspond on left front. Press seams.

TOM KITTEN
ALL-IN-ONE SUIT AND HAT

Tom Kitten was quite unable to jump when walking upon his hind legs in trousers.
THE TALE OF TOM KITTEN

MEASUREMENTS
SUIT

To fit chest	46–48	51–53	56–58	cm
	18–19	*20–21*	*22–23*	*in*
Front, length from	59	67	75	cm
shoulder, approx	*23¼*	*26½*	*29¾*	*in*
(adjustable)				
Inner leg seam	23	28	33	cm
(adjustable)	*9*	*11*	*13*	*in*
Sleeve seam (adjustable)	20	24	28	cm
	8	*9½*	*11*	*in*

N B. Total length is adjustable in leg seam and also in section from crotch to waist.

HAT

Width all round	39	41	43	cm
approx	*15½*	*16¼*	*17*	*in*

MATERIALS
For the set
Hayfield Babykin Double Knit, 40 g balls, Palest Blue (M)

6	6	7

Hayfield Grampian Double Knit, 1 ball (50 g) each Brown (A) and Camel (B).
A pair each 4 mm/No 8 and 3¼ mm/No 10 needles. 4 buttons. 2 press-studs.

TENSION
23 sts and 31 rows to 10 cm/4 in over patt on 4 mm/No 8 needles.

ABBREVIATIONS
K = knit; p = purl; sts = stitches; patt = pattern; g st = garter st; inc = increase, increasing; dec = decrease, decreasing; beg = beginning; tog = together; alt = alternate; sl = slip; foll = following; rep = repeat; 0 = no sts or rows worked on this particular size; cm = centimetres; in = inches.

SUIT

RIGHT LEG
With 3¼ mm needles and M, cast on 40(44, 48) sts loosely.
1st row (right side) – K3, [p2, k2] to last st, k1.

2nd row – K1, [p2, k2] to last 3 sts, p2, k1. Rep these 2 rows for 5 cm/2 in, ending after a 1st row.
Next row – Rib 1(1, 2), [inc once in each of next 4 sts, rib 1] 7(8, 8) times, inc once in each of next 3(1, 3) sts, rib to end. *71(77, 83) sts.*

Change to 4 mm needles and patt thus:
1st row (right side) – P1, [k1, p1] to end.
2nd row – P.
These 2 rows form patt. Continue in patt until work measures 21(26, 31) cm/8¼(10¼, 12¼) in from beg, ending after a p row. (Adjust length here.)

Shape crotch thus:
Taking extra sts into patt, inc 1 st at each end of next 6 rows. *83(89, 95) sts.*
Work 1 row straight. Mark centre of last row.
Now dec 1 st at each end of next 5 rows, then on every alt row until 67(73, 79) sts remain. Continue straight until work measures 12(14, 15) cm/4¾(5½, 6¼) in from marker, ending after a right-side row. (Adjust length here.)

Shape back thus:
1st row – Work across 33 sts, turn.
2nd and every alt row – Sl 1, work to end.
3rd row – Work across 28 sts, turn.
5th row – Work across 23 sts, turn.
7th row – Work across 18 sts, turn.
9th row – Work across 13 sts, turn.
11th row – Work across 8 sts, turn.
12th row – Sl 1, work to end. Cast off all sts loosely.

LEFT LEG
Work as right leg, but working 1 row more before shaping back.

RIGHT FRONT
With 3¼ mm needles and M, cast on 49(52, 55) sts. Work 4 rows in g st.
Next row – K4(5, 7), [inc in next st, k9] 4 times, inc in next st, k to end. *54(57, 60) sts.*

Change to 4 mm needles.
Next row – K.**

Next row – P to last 3 sts, k3. Rep these 2 rows 0(1, 2) times more.

Using separate small balls of yarn for each colour area, otherwise carrying colour/s loosely over back of work when necessary over not more than 5 sts at a time, and twisting yarns on wrong side when changing colour, continue in st st, **working from Chart 8B** (see page 48) thus:
1st row – K, 4M, work 1st row of chart, 7(10, 13)M.
2nd row – P7(10, 13)M, work 2nd row of chart, p1M, k3M.
3rd to 56th rows – Rep 1st and 2nd rows 27 times but working rows 3 to 56 of Chart 8B.

Break A and B. Continue in st st on all sts. **Shape neck** thus:
Next row – K28(29, 30), slip these sts on to a spare needle and leave, k to end.
*** Dec. 1 st at neck edge on next 6 rows, then on the 2 foll alt rows. *18(20, 22) sts.*
Work 0(2, 4) rows straight.

Shape shoulder thus:
Cast off 6(7, 7) sts at beg of next and foll alt row. Work 1 row. Cast off.

LEFT FRONT
Work as right front to ******
Next row – K3, p to end. Rep the last 2 rows 27(28, 29) times more.
Next row – K.

Shape neck thus:
Next row – K3, p25(26, 27), slip these sts on to a spare needle and leave, p to end. Complete as right front, working from ******* to end.

BACK
With 3¼ mm needles and M, cast on 52(58, 64) sts. Work 5 rows in g st, inc 5 sts evenly on last row. *57(63, 69) sts.*

Change to 4 mm needles and, beg with a k row, work 68(72, 76) rows in st st.

Shape shoulders thus:
Cast off 6(7, 7) sts at beg of next 4 rows, then 6(6, 8) sts at beg of foll 2 rows. Slip final 21(23, 25) sts on to a spare needle.

SLEEVES
With 3¼ mm needles and M, cast on 28(32, 32) sts. Work in rib as on legs for 5 cm/2 in, ending after a 1st row.
Next row – Rib 4, *inc in next st, rib 1(3, 2); rep from * to last 4 sts, inc in next st, rib 3. *39(39, 41) sts.*

Change to 4 mm needles and patt as on legs but working in stripes of 4 rows A, 4 rows B, 4 rows M repeated throughout, *at the same time* inc 1 st at each end of 5th row, then on every foll 4th row until there are 53(59, 65) sts, taking extra sts into patt. Work straight until sleeve measures 20(24, 28) cm/8(9½, 11) in or desired length. Cast off loosely with colour of last row.

NECKBAND
First join shoulders. With right side facing, slip sts of right front on to a 3¼ mm needle, rejoin M and using needle holding these sts k up 10(12, 14) sts to right shoulder, k across sts of back, k up 10(12, 14) sts down left side of neck,

finally k across sts on spare needle. *97(105, 113) sts.*
Work 6 rows in g st. Cast off.

TO MAKE UP
Omitting ribbing, press, following pressing instructions on ball band. Stitch cast-off edge of sleeves in position to yoke; join side and sleeve seams. On legs, join front, back and leg seams. Overlapping right front over left front and leaving 25 sts free at outer lower edge of left front, stitch cast-off edge of legs to lower edge of fronts and back, taking care not to stitch tightly. Work 4 buttonhole loops evenly spaced along right front edge, then sew buttons to left front to correspond. Sew press studs to upper and lower corners of left front and corresponding sections of right front. Press seams.

HAT

With 4 mm needles and M, cast on 89(93, 97) sts. Work in patt as legs of suit but working in stripes of [4 rows M, 4 rows A, 4 rows B] 4 times. Break A and B. Continue in M. Beg with a p row, work in st st until hat measures 20(21, 23) cm/8(8½, 9) in from beg, ending after a p row and dec 0(4, 8) sts evenly on last row. *89 sts all sizes.*

Shape crown thus:
1st row – [K9, k2 tog] 8 times, k1.
2nd and every alt row – P.
3rd row – [K8, k2 tog] 8 times, k1.
5th row – [K7, k2 tog] 8 times, k1. Continue in this way, dec 8 sts on every k row until 17 sts remain. Work 1 row. Break yarn. Thread through sts, draw up and fasten off.

Join seam, reversing seam on striped section. Using remainder of yarn in colours as desired, make a pompon and attach to top of crown. Fold striped section over twice to right side.

HUNCA MUNCA
BABY'S HEIRLOOM CHRISTENING DRESS

*The book-case and the bird-cage were rescued from under the coal-box – but
Hunca Munca has got the cradle, and some of Lucinda's clothes.*
THE TALE OF TWO BAD MICE

MEASUREMENTS

To fit chest	46 cm / 18 in	51 cm / 20 in
Length (adjustable)	69 cm / 27 in	70 cm / 27½ in
Sleeve seam	15 cm / 6 in	18 cm / 7 in

MATERIALS

Patons Baby 3 ply Pure Wool,

25 g balls	10	11

or **Patons Fairytale 3 ply**,

50 g balls	6	7

A pair each 3 mm/No 11 and 2¼ mm/No 13 needles. 6 buttons. Approx 1.8 m ready-gathered narrow lace edging, or 3 m if not gathered. 2 skeins Anchor Pearl Cotton 5 for embroidery (optional).

TENSION

Instructions are based on a standard stocking st tension of 32 sts and 40 rows to 10 cm/4 in on 3 mm/No 11 needles.

ABBREVIATIONS

K = knit; p = purl; sts = stitches; patt = pattern; g st = garter st; inc = increase, increasing; dec = decrease, decreasing; yfwd = yarn forward; tog = together; sl = slip; psso = pass slipped st over; m3 = (k1, p1, k1) all into front of next st; beg = beginning; rep = repeat; cm = centimetres; in = inches.

PANEL A (worked over 25 sts)

1st row – P10, k2 tog, yfwd, k1, yfwd, sl 1, k1, psso, p10.
2nd row – K10, p2, k1, p2, k10.
3rd row – P9, k2 tog, yfwd, k1, p1, k1, yfwd, sl 1, k1, psso, p9.
4th row – K9, p2, k3, p2, k9.
5th row – P8, k2 tog, yfwd, k1, p3, k1, yfwd, sl 1, k1, psso, p8.
6th row – K8, p2, k5, p2, k8.
7th row – P7, k2 tog, yfwd, k1, p5, k1, yfwd, sl 1, k1, psso, p7.
8th row – K7, [p2, k7] twice.
9th row – P6, k2 tog, yfwd, k1, p7, k1, yfwd, sl 1, k1, psso, p6.
10th row – K6, p2, k9, p2, k6.
11th row – P5, k2 tog, yfwd, k1, p9, k1, yfwd, sl 1, k1, psso, p5.
12th row – K5, p2, k11, p2, k5.

13th row – P5, *[k1, yfwd] twice, k1 *all* into next st thus making 5 sts out of 1, turn, p5, turn, k5, now slip 2nd, 3rd, 4th and 5th sts on right needle over first st*, p4, k1, yfwd, sl 1, k2 tog, psso, yfwd, k1, p4, work from * to *, p5.
14th row – K10, p5, k10.
15th row – P10, k1, yfwd, sl 1, k2 tog, psso, yfwd, k1, p10.
16th row – As 14th. These 16 rows form panel A.

PANEL B (worked over 33 sts)

1st row – *K1, k2 tog, yfwd, k1, yfwd, sl 1, k1, psso, k1*, p1, [k2 tog] 3 times, [yfwd, k1] 5 times, yfwd, [sl 1, k1, psso] 3 times, p1, work from * to *.
2nd row – P7, k19, p7.
3rd row – *K2, yfwd, sl 1, k2 tog, psso, yfwd, k2*, p1, k17, p1, work from * to *.
4th row – P7, k1, p17, k1, p7.
5th row – K7, p1, [k2 tog] 3 times, [yfwd, k1] 5 times, yfwd, [sl 1, k1, psso] 3 times, p1, k7.
6th row – P7, k19, p7.
7th row – K7, p1, k17, p1, k7.
8th row – P7, k1, p17, k1, p7.
9th to 16th rows – As 1st to 8th.
These 16 rows form panel B.

SLEEVES

With 3 mm needles, cast on 46(50) sts.
1st row (right side) – P.
2nd row – K1, [p3 tog, m3] to last st, k1.
3rd row – P.
4th row – K1, [m3, p3 tog] to last st, k1.
5th to 8th rows – As 1st to 4th.
9th and 10th rows – As 1st and 2nd.**
Next row – P4, [inc in next st, p1] 19(21) times, p4.   *65(71) sts.*
Next row – K.

Change to panel patt thus:
1st row – P13(16), *k1, k2 tog, yfwd, k1, yfwd, sl 1, k1, psso, k1*, work 1st row of panel A, work from * to *, p13(16).
2nd row – K13(16), p7, work 2nd row of panel A, p7, k13(16).
3rd row – P13(16), *k2, yfwd, sl 1, k2 tog, psso, yfwd, k2*, work 3rd row of panel A, work from * to *, p13(16).
4th row – As 2nd, but working 4th row of panel.
5th row – P13(16), k7, work 5th row of panel, k7, p13(16).
6th row – As 2nd, but working 6th row of panel.

7th row – P13(16), k7, work 7th row of panel, k7, p13(16).

8th row – As 2nd, but working 8th row of panel.

9th to 16th rows – As 1st to 8th, but working 9th to 16th rows of panel. These 16 rows form patt.

Continue in patt, inc 1 st at each end of next and every following 6th(8th) row until there are 75(81) sts, taking extra sts into reverse stocking st. Work straight until sleeve measures 15(18) cm / 6(7) in, ending after a wrong-side row.

Keeping patt correct, **shape top** thus:

Cast off 6(7) sts loosely at beg of next 2 rows. Dec 1 st at each end of every right-side row until 51 sts remain, then on every row until 45 sts remain. Cast off.

FRONT

With 2¼ mm needles, cast on 203(211) sts. K 3 rows.

Change to 3 mm needles and panel patt thus:

1st row (right side) – P2(6), [work 1st row of panel A, work 1st row of panel B] 3 times, work 1st row of panel A, p2(6).

2nd row – K2(6), [work 2nd row of panel A, work 2nd row of panel B] 3 times, work 2nd row of panel A, k2(6).

3rd to 16th rows – Rep 1st and 2nd rows 7 times but working 3rd to 16th rows of panels. These 16 rows form patt.

Continue in patt until work measures 60 cm (23½ in) from beg, ending after a wrong-side row. (N B. Length may be adjusted here.)

Keeping patt correct, **shape armholes** thus:

Next 2 rows – K2 tog, [k2 tog, slip 2nd st on right needle over first st] 6(7) times, patt to end. *177(181) sts.*

Mark centre of last row. Now dec 1 st at each end of next 10 rows. *157(161) sts.*

Next row – K1(3), [k2 tog] 77 times, k2(4). *80(84) sts.*

Next row – P19(21), [p2 tog, p1] 14 times, p to end. *66(70) sts.*

Work rows 1 to 10 as at commencement of sleeves.**

Change to 2¼ mm needles and, beg with a k row, work a few rows in stocking st until front measures 5(7) cm / 2¼(2¾) in from marker, ending after a p row.

Shape neck thus:

Next row – K21, turn. Continue on this group. Dec 1 st at neck edge on next 3 rows. *18 sts.*

Work 2 rows straight.

Change to g st and work 4 rows.

Next row – K5, [cast off 2 sts, k4 – including st on needle after cast off] twice, k1.

Next row – K, casting on 2 sts in each place where sts were cast off.

Work 3 more rows in g st. Cast off *loosely*.

With right side facing, slip centre 24(28) sts on to a spare needle. Rejoin yarn to remaining sts. K 1 row. Complete as first side.

BACK

Work as front to **.

Change to 2¼ mm needles and, beg with a k row, work in stocking st until back measures same as front up to g st border.

Change to g st and work 9 rows.

Next row – K22, cast off centre 22(26) sts *loosely*, k to end.

Work 9 rows in g st for button borders on each group of 22 sts. Cast off *loosely*.

FRONT NECKBAND

With 2¼ mm needles, right side facing, k up 46(50) sts *evenly* round front neck including sts on spare needle. K 1 row.

Next row – K3, cast off 2 sts, k to *last* 5 sts, cast off 2 sts, k to end.

Next row – K3, cast on 2 sts, k36(40), cast on 2 sts, k3.

K 5 more rows. Cast off.

TO MAKE UP

With Pearl Cotton 5, embroider flowers in lazy daisy st at centre of approx 7th row of each panel A on skirt and sleeves. Press work *very lightly*, following pressing instructions on ball band. Sew sleeve tops to armholes, noting that front shoulders will overlap button borders of back. Join side and sleeve seams. Sew on buttons. Sew lace to lower edge of sleeves and skirt. Press seams.

PETER RABBIT
MOTHER AND DAUGHTER TUNICS

Peter sat down to rest . . . After a time he began to wander about, going
lippity – lippity – not very fast, and looking all round.
THE TALE OF PETER RABBIT

MEASUREMENTS

To fit	66	71	76	81	86	91	97	cm
chest/bust	*26*	*28*	*30*	*32*	*34*	*36*	*38*	*in*
Length from	44	49	54	60	62	63	65	cm
shoulder, approx	*17½*	*19½*	*21½*	*23½*	*24½*	*25*	*25½*	*in*
Sleeve seam	30	32	37	42	42	42	42	cm
	12	*12¾*	*14½*	*16½*	*16½*	*16½*	*16½*	*in*

MATERIALS
Lister Tahiti Lights, 25 g balls
SWEATER WITHOUT COLLAR
Main colour (M) 10   11   13   15   17   19   21
1 ball each Grey/Brown (A) and Light Tan (B)
SWEATER WITH COLLAR
Main colour (M) 11   13   15   17   19   21   23
1 ball each Grey/Brown (A) and Light Tan (B).
A pair each 5 mm/No 6 and 4 mm/No 8 needles. A few lengths dark brown yarn or Anchor stranded embroidery thread. 2 sequins (optional).

TENSION
16 sts and 22 rows to 10 cm/4 in over st st on 5 mm/No 6 needles.

ABBREVIATIONS
K = knit; p = purl; sts = stitches; st st = stocking st; inc = increase, increasing; dec = decrease, decreasing; foll = following; beg = beginning; alt = alternate; rep = repeat; cm = centimetres; in = inches.

FRONT
With 4 mm needles and M, cast on 55(59, 63, 67, 71, 75, 79) sts. K 4 rows.
Next row (wrong side) – P, inc 6(6, 6, 6, 8, 8, 8) sts evenly across. *61(65, 69, 73, 79, 83, 87) sts.***
Change to 5 mm needles and, beg with a k row, work 6(18, 24, 36, 38, 40, 42) rows in st st.
Using small balls of yarn for each colour area where possible, otherwise carrying colour not in use *loosely* over not more than 5 sts at a time, twisting yarns on wrong side when

changing colour, continue in st st, **working from Chart 13** (see page 78) thus:
1st row – 12(14, 16, 18, 21, 23, 25)M, work 1st row of chart, 12(14, 16, 18, 21, 23, 25)M.
Continue working from Chart 13 as placed on last row until 44th(40th, 42nd, 38th, 38th, 36th, 34th) row has been worked.

Keeping chart correct, **shape square armholes** by casting off 10(11, 12, 12, 12, 13, 14) sts at beg of next 2 rows. *41(43, 45, 49, 55, 57, 59) sts.*
Keeping chart correct, work 19(23, 21, 25, 25, 27, 29) rows straight, thus completing chart.
Continue in M and work 7(7, 9, 9, 9, 11, 11) rows.

Shape neck thus:
Next row – K15(15, 16, 17, 19, 20, 21), turn.
Continue on this group. Dec 1 st at neck edge on next 4 rows. *11(11, 12, 13, 15, 16, 17) sts.*
Work 7(7, 9, 11, 11, 11) rows straight, thus ending at armhole edge.

Shape shoulder thus:
Cast off 4(4, 4, 4, 5, 5, 6) sts at beg of next and foll alt row. Work 1 row. Cast off.

With right side facing, slip next 11(13, 13, 15, 17, 17, 17) sts on a spare needle. Rejoin M. K 1 row. Complete as first side but work 1 row more before shaping shoulder.

BACK
Work as front to **. Change to 5 mm needles and, beg with a k row, work 50(58, 66, 74, 76, 76, 76) rows in st st.

Shape square armholes as on front.
Work 38(42, 44, 48, 50, 54, 56) rows straight.

Shape shoulders thus:
Cast off 4(4, 4, 4, 5, 5, 6) sts at beg of next 4 rows, then 3(3, 4, 5, 5, 6, 5) sts at beg of next 2 rows. Slip final 19(21, 21, 23, 25, 25, 25) sts on a spare needle.

SLEEVES
Begin at top edge. With 5 mm needles and M, cast on 24(28, 24, 28, 24, 28, 32) sts. P 1 row. Continue in st st, casting on 4

CHART 13

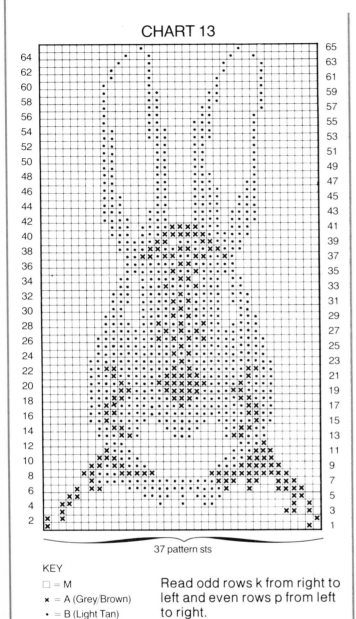

37 pattern sts

KEY

☐ = M
✕ = A (Grey/Brown)
• = B (Light Tan)

Read odd rows k from right to left and even rows p from left to right.

sts at beg of every row until there are 56(60, 64, 68, 72, 76, 80) sts. Mark each end of last row.

Work 14(15, 16, 16, 16, 18, 19) rows straight. Mark each end of last row and centre of last row.

Continue in st st, shaping sleeve by dec 1 st at each end of next and every foll 4th row until 32(36, 36, 38, 40, 44, 46) sts remain.

Work straight until sleeve measures 25(26, 30, 33, 33, 33, 33) cm / 10(10¼, 12, 13, 13, 13, 13) in from centre marker, ending after a k row, and dec 4(8, 4, 6, 8, 12, 10) sts evenly on last row.   *28(28, 32, 32, 32, 32, 36) sts.*

Change to 4 mm needles.
Next row – K1, [p2, k2] to last 3 sts, p2, k1.
Next row – K3, [p2, k2] to last st, k1.
Work 10(12, 12, 18, 18, 18, 18) more rows in rib. Cast off *loosely* in rib.

NECKBAND

First join left shoulder. **With 4 mm needles and M**, right side facing, k across back sts inc 6 sts evenly, k up 12(12, 14, 14, 16, 16, 16) sts down left front neck, k across centre sts inc 4 sts evenly on 1st, 2nd, 3rd and 4th sizes, finally k up 12(12, 14, 14, 16, 16, 16) sts up right front neck.   *64(68, 72, 76, 80, 80, 80) sts.*
Work 13 rows in rib as on cuffs. Cast off very loosely.

ARMHOLE EDGING

First join right shoulder and neckband. **With 4 mm needles and A**, right side facing, k up 60(64, 68, 72, 76, 80, 84) sts evenly along armhole edge omitting cast-off sts. P 2 rows. Cast off *loosely* knitways.

COLLAR (optional)

With 4 mm needles and M, right side facing, cast on 92(96, 100, 104, 108, 112, 116) sts.
Work 22(24, 26, 28, 34, 34, 34) rows in rib as on cuffs.
Keeping rib correct, cast off 6 sts at beg of next 8 rows. Cast off.

TO MAKE UP

Do not press. Embroider eyes, nose and mouth on Peter's face. Sew on sequins for pupils if desired. Stitch shaped cast-on edge of sleeves to armhole edgings. Stitch side edges of sleeves between markers to armhole cast-offs. Join side and sleeve seams. Fold neckband in half to wrong side and hem *loosely* in position. Sew cast-off edge of optional collar to inside of neckband.

SQUIRREL NUTKIN
WOODLAND OVERTOP FOR MOTHER AND DAUGHTER

And to this day, if you meet Nutkin up a tree and ask him a riddle, he will throw sticks at you, and stamp his feet and scold, and shout –
THE TALE OF SQUIRREL NUTKIN

ADULT VERSION – MEASUREMENTS

To fit bust	81	86	91	97	cm
	32	34	36	38	in
Length from shoulder	65	65	66	66	cm
	25¾	25¾	26¼	26¼	in

ADULT VERSION – MATERIALS

Wendy Shetland D K, 50 g balls

Main shade (M)	6	6	7	7

1 ball (50 g) each Rust, Brown and Green.
A pair each 4 mm/No 8 and 3¼ mm/No 10 needles. A few lengths black embroidery thread.

CHILD'S VERSION – MEASUREMENTS

To fit chest	61	66	71	76	cm
	24	26	28	30	in
Length from shoulder	42	46	49	53	cm
	16½	18	19½	21	in

CHILD'S VERSION – MATERIALS

Wendy Shetland D K, 50 g balls

Main shade (M)	3	4	4	4

1 ball (50 g) each Rust, Brown and Green.
A pair each 4 mm/No 8 and 3¼ mm/No 10 needles. A few lengths black embroidery thread.

TENSION

24 sts and 32 rows to 10 cm/4 in over plain st st on 4 mm/No 8 needles, and 28 sts and 28 rows to 10 cm/4 in over patterned st st on 4 mm/No 8 needles.

ABBREVIATIONS

K = knit; p = purl; sts = stitches; st st = stocking st; inc = increase, increasing; dec = decrease, decreasing; tog = together; beg = beginning; alt = alternate; foll = following; rep = repeat; cm = centimetres; in = inches.

FRONT

With 3¼ mm needles and M, cast on 105(111, 117, 123) sts.
1st row (right side) – K2, [p1, k1] to last st, k1.
2nd row –K1, [p1, k1] to end. Rep these 2 rows for 11 cm/4½ in, ending after a 1st row.**
Next row – Rib 4(7, 10, 13), [inc in next st, rib 2] 32 times, inc in next st, rib to end.   *138(144, 150, 156) sts.*

Change to 4 mm needles and, beg with a k row, work 6 rows in st st. Continue in st st, **working from Chart 14 (see page 81)** thus:

(N B. Where possible carry Rust and M loosely over back of work over not more than 5 sts at a time, but use a separate small ball of Brown and Green for each branch, nut and leaf, twisting yarns on wrong side when changing colour.)
1st row – K, 12(14, 16, 18)M, work 1st row of Chart 14 working from right to left, 2(4, 6, 8)M, work 1st row of Chart 14 working from left to right, 12(14, 16, 18)M.
2nd row – P, 12(14, 16, 18)M, work 2nd row of Chart 14 working from right to left, 2(4, 6, 8)M, work 2nd row of Chart 14 working from left to right, p to end in M.
3rd to 49th rows – Rep 1st and 2nd rows 23 times, then 1st row again, but working rows 3 to 49 of chart.
50th row – P in M.
Rep rows 1 to 50 again. Break Rust, Brown and Green.
Next row – K5(8, 11, 14), [K2 tog, k5] 18 times, k2 tog, k to end.   *119(125, 131, 137) sts.*

Work a few rows straight until front measures 53 cm/21 in from beg, ending after a p row.

*** Using a separate small ball of Green for each Oak Leaf and carrying M loosely across back of work over not more than 5 sts at a time, **work Oak Leaves from Chart 14** thus:
1st row – K, 15(17, 19, 21)M, work 17 sts of 1st row of Oak

CHART 14

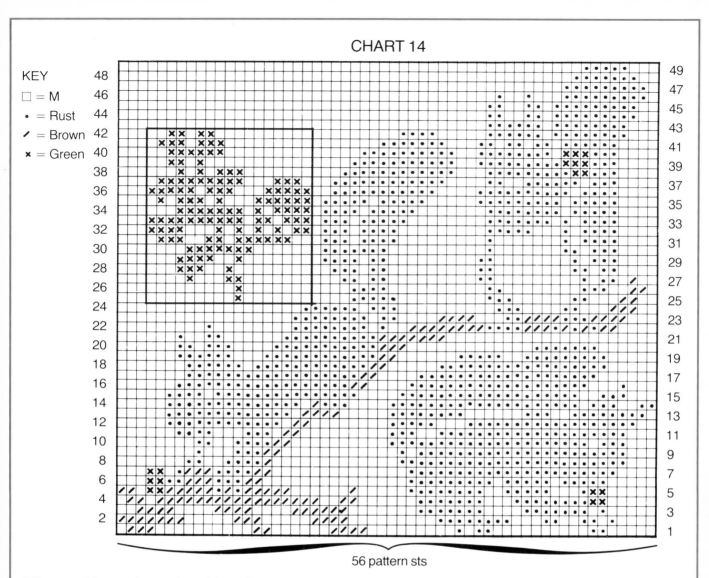

KEY

□ = M
• = Rust
✎ = Brown
✗ = Green

56 pattern sts

When working main section of front from chart 14, ignore heavy line around oak leaf. This has been drawn in to facilitate working of single oak leaves on yoke.

Leaf on Chart 14 working from left to right, 55(57, 59, 61)M, work 17 sts of 1st row of Oak Leaf working from right to left, 15(17, 19, 21)M.

2nd row – P, 15(17, 19, 21)M, work 2nd row of Oak Leaf reading from left to right, 55(57, 59, 61)M, work 2nd row of Oak Leaf reading from right to left, p to end in M.*******

Keeping chart correct, **shape neck** thus:
Next row – K39(41, 43, 45)M, turn.
Continue on this group. Dec 1 st at neck edge on next 5 rows.   *34(36, 38, 40) sts.*
Work 30(30, 34, 34) rows straight, noting that when Oak Leaf is complete all sts should be worked in M.

Shape shoulder thus:
Cast off 11(12, 13, 13) sts at beg of next and foll alt row. Work 1 row. Cast off.

With right side facing, slip centre 41(43, 45, 47) sts on a spare needle. Rejoin M and work 1 row. Complete as first side, working 1 row more before shaping shoulder.

BACK

Work as front to ******
Next row – Rib 6(9, 12, 15), [inc in next st, rib 6] 13 times, inc in next st, rib to end.   *119(125, 131, 137) sts.*

Change to 4 mm needles and, beg with a k row, work in st st until back measures same as front up to start of yoke Oak Leaves, ending after a p row.

Work as front from ******* to *******

Keeping chart correct and noting that when chart is complete all sts should be worked in M, work 36(36, 40, 40) rows.

Shape shoulders thus:
Cast off 11(12, 13, 13) sts at beg of next 4 rows, then 12(12, 12, 14) sts at beg of foll 2 rows. Slip final 51(53, 55, 57) sts on a spare needle.

NECKBAND

First join left shoulder. **With 3¼ mm needles and M**, right side facing, k up 147(151, 161, 165) sts evenly round neck including sts on spare needles. Beg with a 2nd row, work 8 rows in rib as on welt. Cast off in rib.

ARMHOLE BORDERS
First join right shoulder and neckband. Place a marker approx 70(74, 78, 82) rows down from both shoulders at side edges.
With 3¼ mm needles and M, right side facing, k up 103(109, 115, 121) sts evenly between 1 set of markers. Work as neckband.

TO MAKE UP
First embroider squirrel's eyes with black embroidery thread. Omitting ribbing, press, following pressing instructions on ball band. Join side seams and armhole borders. Press seams.

CHILD'S VERSION

FRONT
Commencing with 73(79, 85, 91) sts only, work 22(26, 28, 32) rows in rib as on front of adult version and inc 9 sts evenly on last row. *82(88, 94, 100) sts.*

Change to 4 mm needles and, beg with a k row, work in st st until front measures 13(15, 18, 21) cm/5(6, 7¼, 8¼) in, ending after a p row.
Continue in st st working from **Chart 14** thus:
(NB. Use a separate small ball of yarn for each colour area where possible, otherwise carrying colour not in use *loosely* over not more than 5 sts at a time, twisting yarns on wrong side when changing colour.)
1st row – 13(16, 19, 22)M, work 1st row of Chart 14 working from right to left, 13(16, 19, 22)M.
2nd to 49th rows – Rep 1st row 48 times working rows 2 to 49 of chart, noting that even rows should be worked from left to right and omitting Oak Leaf. Break Rust, Brown and Green.

Work a few rows straight until front measures 33(36, 40, 42) cm/13¼(14¼, 15¾, 16¾) in, ending after a p row.

Using a separate small ball of Green for each Oak Leaf and carrying M loosely over back of work over not more than 5 sts at a time, **work Oak Leaves from Chart 14** thus:
1st row – K, 3(5, 7, 9), work 17 sts of 1st row of Oak Leaf on Chart 14 working from left to right, 42(44, 46, 48)M, work 17 sts of 1st row of Oak Leaf working from right to left, 3(5, 7, 9)M.
2nd row – P, 3(5, 7, 9)M, work 2nd row of Oak Leaf reading from left to right, 42(44, 46, 48)M, work 2nd row of Oak Leaf reading from right to left, p to end in M.***

Keeping chart correct, **shape neck** thus:
Next row – K27(29, 31, 33), turn.
Continue on this group. Dec 1 st at neck edge on next 5 rows. *22(24, 26, 28) sts.*
Work 18(22, 22, 26) rows straight, noting that when Oak Leaf is complete all sts should be worked in M.

Shape shoulder thus:
Cast off 7(8, 9, 9) sts at beg of next and foll alt row. Work 1 row. Cast off.

With right side facing, slip centre 28(30, 32, 34) sts on to a spare needle. Rejoin M and work 1 row. Complete as first side working 1 row more before shaping shoulder.

BACK
Omitting main chart, work as front to ***. Work 24(28, 28, 32) rows, noting that when chart is complete all sts should be worked in M.

Shape shoulders thus:
Cast off 7(8, 9, 9) sts at beg of next 4 rows, then 8(8, 8, 10) sts at beg of foll 2 rows. Slip final 38(40, 42, 44) sts on a spare needle.

NECKBAND
Working 7 rows only and knitting up 103(115, 119, 131) sts only, work as adult version.

ARMHOLE BORDERS
First join right shoulder and neckband. Place a marker approx 54(58, 62, 66) rows down from both shoulders at side edges. Working 7 rows only and knitting up 81(89, 95, 101) sts only, work as adult version.

TO MAKE UP
Make up as adult version.

TOM KITTEN

EDWARDIAN PARTY SWEATER AND SLEEVELESS TOP FOR MOTHER AND DAUGHTER

When the three kittens were ready, Mrs. Tabitha unwisely turned them out into the garden – 'Now keep your frocks clean, children!'
THE TALE OF TOM KITTEN

MEASUREMENTS

To fit	66–71	71–76	79–84	84–89	89–94	cm
chest/bust	26–28	28–30	31–33	33–35	35–37	in
Length from	47	52	56	60	61	cm
shoulder	18½	20½	22	23½	24	in
Sleeve length	40	45	48	53	56	cm
(Sweater)	15¾	17¾	19	21	22	in

MATERIALS

Patons Cotton Perle, 50 g balls

Sweater	10	11	12	13	14
Top	8	9	9	10	10

A pair each 4 mm/No 8 and 3 mm/No 11 needles. A cable needle. A 10 cm/4 in zip-fastener for Sweater.

TENSION

Instructions are based on a standard stocking st tension of 22 sts and 29 rows to 10 cm/4 in on 4 mm/No 8 needles.

ABBREVIATIONS

K = knit; p = purl; sts = stitches; patt = pattern; inc = increase, increasing; dec = decrease, decreasing; beg = beginning; alt = alternate; foll = following; rep = repeat; yfwd = yarn forward; yrn = yarn round needle; sl = slip; psso = pass slipped st over; tog = together; C F = slip next 3 sts on cable needle to front of work, k4, now k3 from cable needle; C B = slip next 4 sts on cable needle to back of work, k3, now k4 from cable needle; cm = centimetres; in = inches.

PANEL (worked over 21 sts)

1st row – C F, p3, yrn, p2 tog, p2, C B.
(N B. alt rows of panel are given in detail in instructions.)
3rd row – K7, p1, p2 tog, yrn, p1, yrn, p2 tog, p1, k7.
5th row – K7, p2 tog, yrn, p3, yrn, p2 tog, k7.
7th row – K7, p2, yrn, p3 tog, yrn, p2, k7.

SWEATER

FRONT

With 3 mm needles, cast on 77(83, 89, 97, 103) sts.
1st row (right side) – K2, [p1, k1] to last st, k1.
2nd row – K1, [p1, k1] to end.
Work 17(21, 25, 29, 33) more rows in rib.
Next row – Rib 3(5, 7, 3, 9), *inc in next st, rib 9(7, 4, 5, 4); rep from * to last 4(6, 7, 4, 9) sts, inc in next st, rib to end. *85(93, 105, 113, 121) sts.*

Change to 4 mm needles and patt thus:
1st row – K2, [yfwd, sl 1, k1, psso, k2] 1(2, 2, 3, 4) times, yfwd, sl 1, k1, psso, k1, *p1(1, 2, 2, 2), work 1st row of panel, p1(1, 2, 2, 2)*, [k2 tog, yfwd, k2] 2(2, 3, 3, 3) times, k2 tog, yfwd, k1, [yfwd, sl 1, k1, psso, k2] 2(2, 3, 3, 3) times, yfwd, sl 1, k1, psso, work from * to *, k1, [k2 tog, yfwd, k2] 2(3, 3, 4, 5) times.
2nd and every alt row – P9(13, 13, 17, 21), *k1(1, 2, 2, 2), p7, k7, p7, k1(1, 2, 2, 2)*, p21(21, 29, 29, 29), work from * to *, p9(13, 13, 17, 21).
3rd row – K1, [k2, yfwd, sl 1, k1, psso] 2(3, 3, 4, 5) times, *p1(1, 2, 2, 2), work 3rd row of panel, p1(1, 2, 2, 2)*, k3, [k2 tog, yfwd, k2] 2(2, 3, 3, 3) times, k1, [yfwd, sl 1, k1, psso, k2] 2(2, 3, 3, 3) times, k1, work from * to*, [k2 tog, yfwd, k2] 2(3, 3, 4, 5) times, k1.
5th row – K2, [k2, yfwd, sl 1, k1, psso] 1(2, 2, 3, 4) times, k3, *p1(1, 2, 2, 2), work 5th row of panel, p1(1, 2, 2, 2)*, k2, [k2 tog, yfwd, k2] 2(2, 3, 3, 3) times, k3, [yfwd, sl 1, k1, psso, k2] 2(2, 3, 3, 3) times, work from * to *, k3, [k2 tog, yfwd, k2] 1(2, 2, 3, 4) times, k2.
7th row – K1, [yfwd, sl 1, k1, psso, k2] 2(3, 3, 4, 5) times, *p1(1, 2, 2, 2), work 7th row of panel, p1(1, 2, 2, 2)*, k1, [k2 tog, yfwd, k2] 2(2, 3, 3, 3) times, k1 [yfwd, sl 1, k1, psso, k2]

2(2, 3, 3, 3) times, yfwd, sl 1, k1, psso, k1, work from * to *, k2, [k2 tog, yfwd, k2] 1(2, 2, 3, 4) times, k2 tog, yfwd, k1.

9th row – K2, [yfwd, sl 1, k1, psso, k2] 1(2, 2, 3, 4) times, yfwd, sl 1, k1, psso, k1, *p1(1, 2, 2, 2), work 1st row of panel, p1(1, 2, 2, 2)*, [k2 tog, yfwd, k2] 2(2, 3, 3, 3) times, k2 tog, yfwd, k1, [yfwd, sl 1, k1, psso, k2] 2(3, 3, 3, 3) times, yfwd, sl 1, k1, psso, work from * to *, k1, [k2 tog, yfwd, k2] 2(3, 3, 4, 5) times.

11th row – As 3rd.

13th row – K2, [k2, yfwd, sl 1, k1, psso] 1(2, 2, 3, 4) times, k3, *p1(1, 2, 2, 2), work 5th row of panel, p1(1, 2, 2, 2)*, k2, [k2 tog, yfwd, k2] 1(1, 2, 2, 2) times, k2 tog, yfwd, k1, yfwd, sl 1, k2 tog, psso, yfwd, k1, [yfwd, sl 1, k1, psso, k2] 2(2, 3, 3, 3) times, work from * to *, k3, [k2 tog, yfwd, k2] 1(2, 2, 3, 4) times, k2.

15th row – As 7th.

16th row – As 2nd.

These 16 rows form patt.

Continue in patt until work measures 24(27, 28, 29, 30) cm / 9½(10½, 11, 11½, 12) in from beg, ending after a wrong-side row.

Keeping patt correct, **shape square armholes** thus:
Cast off 9(13, 13, 17, 21) sts at beg of next 2 rows.   *67(67, 79, 79, 79) sts.* **

Work straight until front measures 42(46, 49, 52, 53) cm / 16½(18, 19½, 20½, 21) in from beg, ending after a wrong-side row.

Shape neck thus:
Next row – Patt 27(27, 32, 32, 32), turn.
Continue on this group. Dec 1 st at neck edge on next 4 rows.   *23(23, 28, 28, 28) sts.*
Work straight until front measures 23(25, 28, 30, 30) cm / 9(10, 11, 12, 12) in from beg of armhole shaping, ending at side edge.

Shape shoulder thus:
Cast off 8(8, 9, 9, 9) sts at beg of next and foll alt row. Work 1 row. Cast off.

With right side facing, slip centre 13(13, 15, 15, 15) sts on to a spare needle. Rejoin yarn to remaining sts and patt 1 row. Complete as first side.

BACK
Work as front to **. Work straight until back measures 12(12, 12, 10, 10) rows *less* than front to shoulder shaping, ending after a wrong-side row.

Divide for zip thus:
Next row – Patt 33(33, 39, 39, 39), cast off next st, patt to end.
Continue on last group. Working 3 sts at inner edge in garter st, work 12(12, 12, 10, 10) rows.

Shape shoulder thus:
Cast off 8(8, 9, 9, 9) sts at beg of next and foll alt row, then 7(7, 10, 10, 10) sts at beg of foll alt row. Work 1 row. Cast off.

With right side facing, rejoin yarn and complete as first side, working 1 row more before shoulder shaping.

SLEEVES
Beg at top with 4 mm needles, cast on 109(117, 125, 133, 133) sts loosely. Purl 1 row. Work in patt thus:
1st row – K3, [yfwd, sl 1, k1, psso, k2] 9(10, 11, 12, 12)

times, yfwd, sl 1, k1, psso, k1, p2, work 1st row of panel, p2, k1, [k2 tog, yfwd, k2] 10(11, 12, 13, 13) times, k1.
2nd and every alt row – P42(46, 50, 54, 54), k2, p7, k7, p7, k2, p42(46, 50, 54, 54).
3rd row – K2, [k2, yfwd, sl 1, k1, psso] 10(11, 12, 13, 13) times, p2, work 3rd row of panel, p2, [k2 tog, yfwd, k2] 10(11, 12, 13, 13) times, k2.
5th row – K1, [yfwd, sl 1, k1, psso, k2] 10(11, 12, 13, 13) times, k1, p2, work 5th row of panel, p2, k3, [k2 tog, yfwd, k2] 9(10, 11, 12, 12) times, k2 tog, yfwd, k1.
7th row – [k2, yfwd, sl 1, k1, psso] 10(11, 12, 13, 13) times, k2, p2, work 7th row of panel, p2, k2, [k2 tog, yfwd, k2] 10(11, 12, 13, 13) times.
8th row – As 2nd.
These 8 rows form patt.
Continue in patt until side edge, not stretched, fits along armhole cast-off edge, ending after a wrong-side row. Mark each end of last row.
Keeping patt correct, dec 1 st at each end of next row then on every foll alt row until 79(83, 87, 99, 103) sts remain, then on every foll 4th row until 57(59, 63, 69, 69) sts remain.
Work straight until sleeve measures 32(37, 38, 43, 46) cm/ 12¾(14¾, 15, 17, 18) in from beg, measured at centre, ending after a right-side row.
Next row – P8(9, 9, 8, 10), [p2 tog] 20(20, 22, 26, 24) times, p to end. *37(39, 41, 43, 45) sts.*

Change to 3 mm needles and work 23(23, 31, 31, 31) rows in rib as on welt. Now cast off to form picot thus:
Cast off 2 sts, *slip st on right needle back on to left needle, cast on 2 sts, cast off 5 sts; rep from * until no sts remain.

FRILL (4 pieces alike)
With 3 mm needles cast on 45(49, 53, 57, 57) sts. K1(1, 1, 3, 3) rows.
Next row – K1, inc once in every st to end. *89(97, 105, 113, 113) sts.*

Change to 4 mm needles and work in patt thus:
1st row – K1, [yfwd, k2, sl 1, k2 tog, psso, k2, yfwd, k1] to end.
2nd, 4th and 6th rows – K1, p to last st, k1.
3rd row – K2, [yfwd, k1, sl 1, k2 tog, psso, k1, yfwd, k3] to last 7 sts, yfwd, k1, sl 1, k2 tog, psso, k1, yfwd, k2.
5th row – K3, [yfwd, sl 1, k2 tog, psso, yfwd, k5] to last 6 sts, yfwd, sl 1, k2 tog, psso, yfwd, k3.
7th row – K4, [yfwd, sl 1, k1, psso, k6] to last 5 sts, yfwd, sl 1, k1, psso, k3.
8th row – As 2nd.
Rep 1st to 7th rows once. Knit 2 rows. Cast off to form picot as on sleeves.

NECKBAND
First join shoulders firmly. **With 3 mm needles**, right side facing, k up 63(67, 71, 75, 75) sts evenly round neck including sts on spare needle. Beg with a 2nd row, work 14(14, 14, 16, 16) rows in rib as on welt. Cast off to form picot as on sleeves.

TO MAKE UP
Omitting ribbing, press, following pressing instructions on ball band. Stitch cast-on edge of sleeves to side edges of armholes, and marked sections of sleeves to armhole cast-offs. Press seams. Join one side edge of frill pieces to form two long strips. Stitch cast-on edge of frills to armhole seams, stitching side edges to armhole cast-off seams. Join side and sleeve seams. Sew in zip. Press side and sleeve seams.

TOP

FRONT AND BACK (2 pieces alike)
Work as front of Sweater until 16th row of patt has been worked. Continue straight in patt until work measures 42(46, 49, 52, 53) cm/16½(18, 19½, 20½, 21) in from beg, ending after a wrong-side row.

Shape neck thus:
Next row – Patt 32(35, 37, 40, 44), cast off centre 21(23, 31, 33, 33) sts, patt to end. Continue on last group. Dec 1 st at neck edge on next 3 rows, then on 3 foll alt rows. *26(29, 31, 34, 38) sts.*
Continue straight until front measures 47(52, 56, 60, 61) cm/18½(20½, 22, 23½, 24) in from beg, ending at side edge.
Shape shoulder as on front of Sweater. With wrong side facing, rejoin yarn to remaining sts. Complete as first side.

FRILL (2 pieces alike)
Commencing with 81(85, 93, 97, 101) sts, and noting that there will be 161(169, 185, 193, 201) sts after inc row, work as Sweater frill.

NECKBAND
First join left shoulder. **With 3 mm needles**, right side facing, k up 80(92, 98, 115, 115) sts evenly round neck. Knit 2 rows. Cast off to form picot as on sleeves of Sweater.

TO MAKE UP
Press as Sweater. Join right shoulder and neckband. Leaving approx 17(18, 20, 21, 23) cm/6½(7, 8, 8½, 9) in free for armholes, join side seams. Join side edges of frills to form two rings. Stitch cast-on edges of frills to armholes. Press seams.

SHEAF OF CORN

OVERTOP AND WAISTCOAT FOR MOTHER AND DAUGHTER

Intery, mintery, cuttery, corn,   Five geese in a flock,
Apple seed and apple thorn;   Sit and stand by a spring,
Wine, brier, limber-lock,   O-U-T, and in again.

BEATRIX POTTER'S NURSERY RHYME BOOK

MEASUREMENTS

To fit	71	76	81	86	91	97	102	cm
chest/bust	28	30	32	34	36	38	40	in

OVERTOP
Length from

shoulder	58	61	63	66	66	67	67	cm
approx	23	24	25	26	26	26½	26½	in

WAISTCOAT
Length from

shoulder	63	66	69	71	71	72	72	cm
approx	25	26	27	28	28	28½	28½	in

MATERIALS

Patons Beehive Chunky or **Beehive Chunky Twirl**, 50 g balls

OVERTOP	8	8	8	9	9	10	10
WAISTCOAT	11	11	11	12	12	12	13

A pair each 5½ mm/No 5 and 4½ mm/No 7 needles. A cable needle. 7 buttons for Waistcoat.

TENSION

16 sts and 22 rows to 10 cm/4 in over stocking st on 5½ mm/No 5 needles.

ABBREVIATIONS

K = knit; p = purl; sts = stitches; tw2 = slip next st, k1, pass slipped st over st just knitted and k into back of it; patt = pattern; inc = increase, increasing; dec = decrease, decreasing; beg = beginning; alt = alternate; rep = repeat; CRF = slip next st on cable needle to front of work, k1, p1, now k1 from cable needle; tog = together; CB = slip next 2 sts on cable needle to back of work, k1, now k2 from cable needle; CF = slip next st on cable needle to front of work, k2, now k1 from cable needle; m1 = make 1 by picking up and purling into back of horizontal strand lying before next st; m3 = make 3 thus: [k1, p1, k1] all into front of next st; foll = following; cm = centimetres; in = inches.

CABLE PANEL (worked over 9 sts)

1st row – CRF, [p1, k1] 3 times.
2nd, 4th and 6th rows – P1, [k1, p1] 4 times.

3rd row – K1, p1, CRF, [p1, k1] twice.
5th row – [K1, p1] twice, CRF, p1, k1.
7th row – [K1, p1] 3 times, CRF.
8th row – As 2nd.
These 8 rows form cable panel.

SHEAF OF CORN PANEL (worked over 29 sts)

1st row – P6, p2 tog, CB, p1, m1, [k1, p1] twice, k1, m1, p1, CF, p2 tog, p6.
2nd row – K7, p3, k2, [p1, k1] 3 times, k1, p3, k7.
3rd row – P5, p2 tog, CF, p1, m1, p1, [k1, p1] 3 times, m1, p1, CB, p2 tog, p5.
4th and every foll alt row to 34th row – Work across 29 sts, knitting all k sts and m1 sts and purling all p sts (including CB and CF sts).
5th row – P4, p2 tog, CB, p1, m1, p2, [k1, p1] 3 times, p1, m1, p1, CF, p2 tog, p4.
7th row – P3, p2 tog, CF, p1, m1, p3, [k1, p1] 3 times, p2, m1, p1, CB, p2 tog, p3.
9th row – P2, p2 tog, CB, p1, m1, p4, [k1, p1] 3 times, p3, m1, p1, CF, p2 tog, p2.
11th row – P1, p2 tog, [k1, p1] twice, m1, p1, p2 tog, CB, p1, m1, k1, m1, p1, CF, p2 tog, p1, m1, [p1, k1] twice, p2 tog, p1.
13th row – P2 tog, [k1, p1] twice, m1, p1, p2 tog, CF, p1, m1, p1, k1, p1, m1, p1, CB, p2 tog, p1, m1, [p1, k1] twice, p2 tog.
15th row – [P1, k1] twice, p2, p2 tog, CB, p1, m1, p2, k1, p2, m1, p1, CF, p2 tog, p2, [k1, p1] twice.
17th row – P5, p2 tog, CF, p1, m1, p3, k1, p3, m1, p1, CB, p2 tog, p5.
19th row – P4, p2 tog, CB, p1, m1, p4, k1, p4, m1, p1, CF, p2 tog, p4.
21st row – P3, p2 tog, [k1, p1] twice, m1, p4, CF, p4, m1, [p1, k1] twice, p2 tog, p3.
23rd row – P2, p2 tog, [k1, p1] twice, m1, p5, CB, p5, m1, [p1, k1] twice, p2 tog, p2.
25th row – P3, k1, p1, k1, p7, CF, p7, k1, p1, k1, p3.
27th row – P3, k1, p1, k1, p7, CB, p7, k1, p1, k1, p3.
29th row – As 25th.
31st, 33rd and 35th rows – P13, k1, p1, k1, p13.
36th row – K11, k2 tog, p1, k1, p1, k2 tog, k11.   27 sts.
These 36 rows form the Sheaf of Corn panel.

OVERTOP

FRONT
With 4½ mm needles, cast on 66(70, 74, 78, 82, 86, 90) sts.
1st row (right side) – K1, p1, [tw2, p2] to last 4 sts, tw2, p1, k1.
2nd row – K2, [p2, k2] to end.
Work 21 more rows in rib.
Next row – Rib 3(5, 7, 3, 5, 7, 3), *inc in next st, rib 4(4, 4, 5, 5, 5, 6); rep from * to last 3(5, 7, 3, 5, 7, 3) sts, inc in next st, rib to end. *79(83, 87, 91, 95, 99, 103) sts.*

Change to 5½ mm needles and patt thus:
1st row – P2, *k1, p6, k1, p4(5, 6, 7, 8, 9, 10), k1, p6, k1*, p13(14, 15, 16, 17, 18, 19), k1, [p1, k1] 4 times, p13(14, 15, 16, 17, 18, 19), work from * to *, p2.
2nd row – K2, *p1, k1, p3 tog, m3, k1, p1, k4(5, 6, 7, 8, 9, 10), p1, k1, m3, p3 tog, k1, p1*, k13(14, 15, 16, 17, 18, 19), p1, [k1, p1] 4 times, k13(14, 15, 16, 17, 18, 19), work from * to*, k2.
3rd row – As 1st.
4th row – K2, *p1, k1, m3, p3 tog, k1, p1, k4(5, 6, 7, 8, 9, 10), p1, k1, p3 tog, m3, k1, p1*, k13(14, 15, 16, 17, 18, 19), p1, [k1, p1] 4 times, k13(14, 15, 16, 17, 18, 19), work from * to *, k2.
These 4 rows form basic patt for lower section of front.
Patt 8(10, 16, 18, 18, 18, 18) more rows.

** Work centre cable patt thus:
1st row – Patt 35(37, 39, 41, 43, 45, 47), work 1st row of cable panel, patt 35(37, 39, 41, 43, 45, 47).
2nd to 8th rows – Rep 1st row 7 times but working rows 2 to 8 of cable panel.
Now working 9 centre sts all in rib as at commencement and remainder as before, work 8 rows.** Rep the last 16 rows once.

*** Work Sheaf of Corn panel thus:
1st row – Patt 25(27, 29, 31, 33, 35, 37), work 1st row of Sheaf of Corn panel, patt 25(27, 29, 31, 33, 35, 37).
2nd to 36th rows – Rep 1st row 35 times but working rows 2 to 36 of panel. *77(81, 85, 89, 93, 97, 101) sts.****
Work 8 rows working centre sts all in reverse stocking st.

Keeping patt correct, **shape neck** thus:
Next row – Patt 30(31, 33, 34, 36, 37, 39), turn.
Continue on this group. Dec 1 st at neck edge on next 5 rows. *25(26, 28, 29, 31, 32, 34) sts.*
**** Work straight until front measures 7(9, 9, 10, 10, 11, 11) cm/3(3½, 3½, 4, 4, 4½, 4½) in from beg of neck shaping, ending at side edge.

Shape shoulder thus:
Cast off 8(9, 9, 10, 10, 11, 11) sts at beg of next and foll alt row.
Work 1 row. Cast off.********

With right side facing, slip centre 17(19, 19, 21, 21, 23, 23) sts on to a spare needle. Rejoin yarn to remaining sts. Patt 1 row. Complete as first side.

BACK
Omitting neck shaping, work as front to shoulder shaping, ending after a wrong-side row.

Shape shoulders by casting off 8(9, 9, 10, 10, 11, 11) sts at beg of next 4 rows, then 9(8, 10, 9, 11, 10, 12) sts at beg of next 2

rows. Slip remaining 27(29, 29, 31, 31, 33, 33) sts on to a spare needle.

NECKBAND
First join left shoulder. With 4½ mm needles, right side facing, k up 78(86, 86, 94, 94, 102, 102) sts evenly round neck, including sts on spare needles. Beg with a 2nd row, work 6 rows in rib as on welt. Cast off evenly in rib.

ARMBANDS
First join right shoulder and neckband. ****Place a marker on side edges 38(40, 43, 45, 48, 50, 53) rows down from each shoulder. With 4½ mm needles, right side facing, k up 70(74, 78, 82, 86, 90, 94) sts evenly between 1 set of markers. Work as neckband.

TO MAKE UP
Do not press. Join side seams and armbands.******

WAISTCOAT

RIGHT FRONT
With 4½ mm needles, cast on 42(46, 46, 50, 50, 54, 54) sts.
Work 12 rows in rib as on front of Overtop, dec 1(3, 1, 3, 1, 3, 1) sts evenly on last row. *41(43, 45, 47, 49, 51, 53) sts.***

Change to 5½ mm needles and patt thus:
1st row – P11(12, 13, 14, 15, 16, 17), k1, [p1, k1] 4 times, p11(12, 13, 14, 15, 16, 17), k1, p6, k1, p2.

2nd row – K2, p1, k1, p3 tog, m3, k1, p1, k11(12, 13, 14, 15, 16, 17), p1, [k1, p1] 4 times, k to end.

3rd row – As 1st.

4th row – K2, p1, k1, m3, p3 tog, k1, p1, k11(12, 13, 14, 15, 16, 17), p1, [k1, p1] 4 times, k to end. These 4 rows form basic patt for lower section of right front.

Patt 20(22, 28, 30, 30, 30, 30) rows more.

Work cable patt thus:

1st row – P11(12, 13, 14, 15, 16, 17), work 1st row of cable panel, work to end.

2nd row – Work across 21(22, 23, 24, 25, 26, 27) sts, work 2nd row of cable panel, k to end.

3rd to 8th rows – Rep 1st and 2nd rows 3 times but working rows 3 to 8 of cable panel.

Now working the 9 sts of cable panel all in rib as at commencement and remainder as before, work 8 rows.

Rep the last 16 rows twice more.

Work Sheaf of Corn panel thus:

1st row – P1(2, 3, 4, 5, 6, 7), work 1st row of Sheaf of Corn panel, work to end.

2nd row – Work across 11(12, 13, 14, 15, 16, 17) sts, work 2nd row of **Sheaf of Corn** panel, k to end.

***3rd to 36th rows** – Rep 1st and 2nd rows 17 times but working rows 3 to 36 of panel. *39(41, 43, 45, 47, 49, 51) sts.*

Working 8 side border patt sts as before and remainder in reverse stocking st, work 2 rows.

Shape neck thus:

Cast off 9(10, 10, 11, 11, 12, 12) sts at beg of next row. Dec 1 st at neck edge on next 5 rows. *25(26, 28, 29, 31, 32, 34) sts.*

Work as front of Overtop from **** to ****.

LEFT FRONT

Work as right front to **.

Change to 5½ mm needles and patt thus:

1st row – P2, k1, p6, k1, p11(12, 13, 14,15, 16, 17), k1, [p1, k1] 4 times, p11(12, 13, 14, 15, 16, 17).

2nd row – K11(12, 13, 14, 15, 16, 17), p1, [k1, p1] 4 times, k11(12, 13, 14, 15, 16, 17), p1, k1, m3, p3 tog, k1, p1, k2.

3rd row – As 1st.

4th row – K11(12, 13, 14, 15, 16, 17), p1, [k1, p1] 4 times, k11(12, 13, 14, 15, 16, 17), p1, k1, p3 tog, m3, k1, p1, k2. Patt 20(22, 28, 30, 30, 30, 30) rows more.

Work cable patt thus:

1st row – Patt 21(22, 23, 24, 25, 26, 27), work 1st row of cable panel, p to end.

2nd row – K11(12, 13, 14, 15, 16, 17), work 2nd row of cable panel, work to end.

3rd to 8th rows – Rep 1st and 2nd rows 3 times but working rows 3 to 8 of cable panel.

Now working the 9 sts of cable panel all in rib as at commencement and remainder as before, work 8 rows.

Rep the last 16 rows twice more.

Work Sheaf of Corn panel thus:

1st row – Work across 11(12, 13, 14, 15, 16, 17) sts, work 1st row of Sheaf of Corn panel, p to end.

2nd row – K1(2, 3, 4, 5, 6, 7), work 2nd row of Sheaf of Corn panel, work to end.

Complete to match right front working from *** to end, noting that 3 rows in place of 2 should be worked before shaping neck.

BACK

With 4½ mm needles, cast on 82(86, 90, 94, 98, 102, 106) sts. Work 12 rows in rib as on fronts, dec 3 sts evenly on last row. *79(83, 87, 91, 95, 99, 103) sts.*

Change to 5½ mm needles and patt thus:

1st row – P2, k1, p6, k1, p25(27, 29, 31, 33, 35, 37), k1, [p1, k1] 4 times, p to last 10 sts, k1, p6, k1, p2.

2nd row – K2, p1, k1, p3 tog, m3, k1, p1, k25(27, 29, 31, 33, 35, 37), p1, [k1, p1] 4 times, k to last 10 sts, p1, k1, m3, p3 tog, k1, p1, k2.

3rd row – As 1st.

4th row – K2, p1, k1, m3, p3 tog, k1, p1, k25(27, 29, 31, 33, 35, 37), p1, [k1, p1] 4 times, k to last 10 sts, p1, k1, p3 tog, m3, k1, p1, k2.

Patt 20(22, 28, 30, 30, 30, 30) rows more.

Work as front of Overtop from ** to **. Rep the last 16 rows twice more.

Work as front of Overtop from *** to ***.

Working centre sts all in reverse stocking st, work straight until back measures same as fronts, ending after a wrong-side row.

Shape shoulders as on back of Overtop.

NECKBAND

First join shoulders. With 4½ mm needles, right side facing, k up 74(82, 82, 90, 90, 98, 98) sts evenly round neck. Work as Overtop neckband but casting off firmly.

ARMBANDS

Work as Overtop armbands from ** to end.

FRONT BORDERS

With 4½ mm needles, cast on 9 sts.

1st row (right side) – K2, [p1, k1] 3 times, k1.

2nd row – K1, [p1, k1] to end.

Rep these 2 rows until strip, when slightly stretched, fits up front edge to top of neckband. Cast off firmly in rib. Mark position on border for 7 buttons, 1st to be level with top of welt, last in 3rd/4th rows from top and remaining 5 spaced evenly between.

Work second strip as first but with the addition of holes to match markers thus:

1st row (right side) – Rib 3, cast off 3 sts in rib, rib to end.

2nd row – In rib, casting on 3 sts over those cast off.

TO MAKE UP

Make up as overtop to **. Sew on borders and buttons.

90

SHEAF OF CORN
BOMBER JACKET AND BERET FOR MOTHER AND DAUGHTER

'I am sure you will never want to live in town again,' said Timmy Willie.
THE TALE OF JOHNNY TOWN-MOUSE

MEASUREMENTS
JACKET

To fit chest/bust	76	81	86	91	97	102 cm
	30	*32*	*34*	*36*	*38*	*40 in*
Length at centre	52	56	60	60	62	63 cm
back, excluding	*20½*	*22*	*23½*	*23½*	*24½*	*25 in*
neckband, approx						
Sleeve seam, approx	33	39	46	46	46	46 cm
	13	*15½*	*18*	*18*	*18*	*18 in*

BERET, to fit head size 54–57 cm / 21½–22½ in

MATERIALS
Argyll Fluffy Chunky, 100 g balls

JACKET	4	5	5	6	6	6

BERET, 1 ball (100 g)
A pair 5½ mm/No 5 and 4½ mm/No 7 needles. A cable needle. 8 buttons for Jacket.

TENSION
15 sts and 22 rows to 10 cm/4 in over stocking st on 5½ mm/No 5 needles.

ABBREVIATIONS
Cable Panel and **Sheaf of Corn Panel**, see page 87.

JACKET

RIGHT HALF
Begin at cuff. **With 4½ mm needles**, cast on 26(30, 30, 34, 34, 34) sts.
1st row (right side) – K1, p1, [tw2, p2] to last 4 sts, tw2, p1, k1.
2nd row – K2, [p2, k2] to end.
Rep these 2 rows for 10 cm/4 in, ending after a 2nd row.
Next row – K, inc once in every st.   *52(60, 60, 68, 68, 68) sts.*
Next row – P, inc 7(3, 7, 1, 5, 7) sts evenly across the row.   *59(63, 67, 69, 73, 75) sts.*

Change to 5½ mm needles and patt thus:
1st row – K2(3, 4, 5, 6, 7), p23(24, 25, 25, 26, 26), k1, [p1, k1] 4 times, p23(24, 25, 25, 26, 26), k2(3, 4, 5, 6, 7).
2nd row – P2(3, 4, 5, 6, 7), k1, [p3 tog, m3] twice, k14(15, 16, 16, 17, 17), p1, [k1, p1] 4 times, k14(15, 16, 16, 17, 17), [m3, p3 tog] twice, k1, p to end.
3rd row – As 1st.
4th row – P2(3, 4, 5, 6, 7), k1, [m3, p3 tog] twice, k14(15, 16, 16, 17, 17), p1, [k1, p1] 4 times, k14(15, 16, 16, 17, 17), [p3 tog, m3] twice, k1, p to end.
These 4 rows form basic patt with side panels in blackberry st.
Work 16(10, 8, 8, 8, 8) more rows in patt.

Work cable panel patt thus:
1st row – Patt 25(27, 29, 30, 32, 33), work 1st row of cable panel, patt to end.
2nd to 8th rows – Rep 1st row 7 times but working rows 2 to 8 of cable panel.
Keeping blackberry st correct, work 10 rows in basic patt as at commencement.

2nd size only
Rep the last 18 rows once more.

3rd, 4th, 5th and 6th sizes only
Rep the last 18 rows twice more.

Work Sheaf of Corn panel thus:
1st row – Patt 15(17, 19, 20, 22, 23), work 1st row of Sheaf of Corn panel, patt 15(17, 19, 20, 22, 23).
2nd row – As 1st, but working 2nd row of panel.

Continue with Sheaf of Corn panel, working rows 3 to 14 of panel, *at the same time* **shape sleeve** by inc 1 st at each end of next row, then the 3 foll right-side rows, then on next 5 rows.   *77(81, 85, 87, 91, 93) sts.*
Keeping panel correct, cast on 25(29, 33, 33, 33, 34) sts at beg of next 2 rows.   *127(139, 151, 153, 157, 161) sts.*
Work new blackberry st bands thus:
1st row – K12(15, 18, 18, 18, 20), p10, k14(16, 18, 19, 20, 20),

working 17th row of panel, work to *last* 36(41, 46, 47, 48, 50) sts, k14(16, 18, 19, 20, 20), p10, k12(15, 18, 18, 18, 20)
2nd row – P12(15, 18, 18, 18, 20), k1, [p3 tog, m3] twice, k1, p14(16, 18, 19, 20, 20), work to *last* 36(41, 46, 47, 48, 50) sts, p14(16, 18, 19, 20, 20), k1, [m3, p3 tog] twice, k1, p to end.
3rd row – As 1st row but working 19th row of panel.
4th row – P12(15, 18, 18, 18, 20), k1, [m3, p3 tog] twice, k1, p14(16, 18, 19, 20, 20), work to *last* 36(41, 46, 47, 48, 50) sts, p14(16, 18, 19, 20, 20), k1, [p3 tog, m3] twice, k1, p to end.
Continue in patt as on these 4 rows until 36th row of Sheaf of Corn panel has been worked.   *125(137, 149, 151, 155, 159) sts.*
Working centre sts all in reverse stocking st, work 14(16, 16, 20, 22, 22) rows.

Shape neck thus:
Next row – Work across 53(57, 61, 62, 64, 66) sts, cast off 11(13, 15, 15, 15, 15) sts loosely, work to end.
Continue on last group and work 13(13, 15, 15, 15, 17) rows straight. Cast off loosely.

With wrong side facing, rejoin yarn to remaining sts. Dec 1 st at neck edge on next 3 rows.   *50(54, 58, 59, 61, 63) sts.*
Work 8(8, 10, 10, 10, 12) rows straight. Cast off loosely.

LEFT HALF
Work as right half but working 1 row less before shaping neck, and noting that right side will be facing when rejoining yarn for front section of neck.

WELT
First join centre-back seam, side and sleeve seams. **With 4½ mm needles**, right side facing, k up 134(142, 150, 158, 166, 174) sts *evenly* along lower edge. Beg with a 2nd row, work in rib as on cuffs for 11 cm/4½ in, ending after a 1st row. Cast off *loosely* in rib.

NECKBAND
With 4½ mm needles, right side facing, k up 66(74, 86, 86, 86, 90) sts evenly round neck. Beg with a 2nd row, work 8 rows in rib as on welt. Cast off firmly in rib.

BORDERS
With 4½ mm needles, cast on 10 sts.
1st row – K1, tw2, p1, k2, p1, tw2, k1.
2nd row – K1, (p2, k1) 3 times.
Rep these 2 rows until strip when slightly stretched fits up front edge to top of neckband, ending after a 1st row. Cast off firmly. Sew border to left front.
Mark position on border for 8 buttons, 1st to be in 3rd and 4th rows, 3rd level with top of welt, 2nd one spaced evenly between 1st and 3rd, 8th to be in 3rd/4th rows from top and remaining 4 spaced between 3rd and 8th.

Work 2nd strip as 1st, but with holes to match markers thus:
1st row – Rib 4, cast off 2 sts, rib to end.
2nd row – In rib, casting on 2 over those cast off.

TO MAKE UP
Do not press. Sew on buttonhole border and buttons.

BERET

TO MAKE
With 4½ mm needles, cast on 81 sts.
1st row (right side) – K2, [p1, k1] to last st, k1.
2nd row – K1, [p1, k1] to end.
Work 4 more rows in rib, inc 8 sts evenly on last row.   *89 sts.*

Change to 5½ mm needles and patt thus:
1st row – P1, [C B, p8] 8 times.
2nd row – [K8, p3] 8 times, k1.
3rd row – P1, [C F, p8] 8 times.
4th row – As 2nd. These 4 rows form basic patt of narrow cable panels and reverse stocking st.

Shape thus:
1st row – P1, [C B, p1, m1, p6, m1, p1] 8 times.
2nd row – [K10, p3] 8 times, k1.
3rd and 4th rows – Keeping patt correct, work 2 rows.
5th row – P1, [C B, p1, m1, p8, m1, p1] 8 times.
6th row – [K12, p3] 8 times, k1.
7th and 8th rows – As 3rd and 4th.
9th row – P1, [C B, p1, m1, p10, m1, p1] 8 times.   *137 sts.*

Keeping cables correct, work straight until beret measures 14 cm/5¾ in from beg, ending after a wrong-side row.

Shape crown thus:
1st row – P1, [patt 3, p2 tog, p12] 8 times.
2nd and every alt row – Work to end, knitting every k st and purling every p st.
3rd row – P1, [patt 3, p2 tog, p11] 8 times.
5th row – P1, [patt 3, p2 tog, p10] 8 times.
Continue in this way, dec 8 sts on every right-side row until 41 sts remain. Work 1 row. Break yarn and thread through sts, draw up and fasten off securely.

Do not press. Join seam. Make a 41 cm/16 in long twisted cord (see page 111). Catch centre of cord to centre of crown and tie in a bow. Make 2 tassels and stitch one to each end of cord.

HERDWICK
CAPE JACKETS FOR MOTHER AND DAUGHTER

Shepherdess of fields on high,
Drive in your thousand sheep!
Flocks that stray across the sky,
And clouds that sail the deep!
BEATRIX POTTER'S NURSERY RHYME BOOK

MEASUREMENTS

To fit chest/bust	66–74	76–84	86–94	cm
	26–29	30–33	34–37	*in*
Centre back length	54	67	79	cm
from shoulder,	21½	26½	31	*in*
excluding				
neckband, approx				
Nape of neck to base	53	62	71	cm
of cuff, approx	21	24½	28	*in*

MATERIALS

Lister Genuine Herdwick or
Lister Pure Wool Aran,

50 g balls	16	23	27

A pair long 5 mm/No 6 and 4 mm/No 8 needles. A cable needle. A 4½ mm/No 7 crochet hook.

TENSION

18 sts and 22 rows to 10 cm/4 in over stocking st on 5 mm/No 6 needles.

ABBREVIATIONS

K = knit; p = purl; sts = stitches; patt = pattern; inc = increase, increasing; dec = decrease, decreasing; alt = alternate; foll = following; rep = repeat; tw2 = slip 1, k1, pass slipped st over st just knitted and k into back of it; C B = slip next st on cable needle to back of work, k1, now k1 from cable needle; CF = slip next st on cable needle to front of work, k1, now k1 from cable needle; tog = together; m3 = [k1, p1, k1] all into front of next st thus making 3 sts out of 1; cm = centimetres; in = inches.

RIGHT FRONT

With 5 mm needles, cast on 65(65, 75) sts. Work in patt, shaping side edge thus:
1st row – P5, tw2, p8, tw2, p3, C B, CF, p8, C B, CF, p3, [tw2, p8] 2(2, 3) times, tw2, p3, inc purlways in last st.
2nd row – Inc knitways in first st, k4, [p2, k8] 2(2, 3) times, p2, k3, p4, [p3 tog, m3] twice, p4, k3, p2, k8, p2, k5.
3rd row – P5, tw2, p8, tw2, p3, CF, C B, p8, CF, C B, p3,

[tw2, p8] 2(2, 3) times, tw2, p5, inc purlways in last st.
4th row – Inc knitways in first st, k6, [p2, k8] 2(2, 3) times, p2, k3, p4, [m3, p3 tog] twice, p4, k3, p2, k8, p2, k5.
** On these 4 rows 1 repeat of blackberry st and cable panel with tw2, p8 ribs has been worked.

Keeping panel correct and working extra sts into tw2, p8 rib, continue inc at side edge on every row until there are 84(98, 106) sts, then on every foll alt row until there are 90(103, 118) sts, finally on every foll 4th row until there are 94(108, 124) sts.*** Work 1 row straight.

Keeping side edge straight, **shape front slope** thus:
Dec 1 st at front edge on next row, then on every foll 4th row until 82(94, 108) sts remain.
Work 9(13, 13) rows straight. Cast off.

LEFT FRONT

With 5 mm needles, cast on 65(65, 75) sts. Work in patt, shaping side edge thus:
1st row – Inc purlways in first st, p3, *[tw2, p8] 2(2, 3) times, tw2, p3, C B, CF, p8, C B, CF, p3, tw2, p8, tw2, p5.
2nd row – K5, p2, k8, p2, k3, p4, [m3, p3 tog] twice, p4, k3, [p2, k8] 2(2, 3) times, p2, k4, inc knitways in last st.
3rd row – Inc purlways in first st, p5, work as 1st row from * to end but working CF in place of C B, and C B in place of CF.
4th row – K5, p2, k8, p2, k3, p4, [p3 tog, m3] twice, p4, k3, [p2, k8] 2(2, 3) times, p2, k6, inc knitways in last st.
Complete as right front working from ** to end.

LEFT BACK

Work as right front to ***. Work 71(83, 91) rows straight. Cast off. (N B. Back is longer than front to allow for the saddle shoulder.)

RIGHT BACK

Work as left front until 4th row has been worked. Complete to match left back, reversing shapings.

RIGHT SADDLE SHOULDER AND CUFF

Begin at front neck edge. **With 5 mm needles**, cast on 18 sts.

1st row – P1, CB, CF, p8, CB, CF, p1.
2nd row – K1, p4, [p3 tog, m3] twice, p4, k1.
3rd row – P1, CF, CB, p8, CF, CB, p1.
4th row – K1, p4, [m3, p3 tog] twice, p4, k1.
Rep these 4 rows until strip measures 39(46, 52) cm/15½(18, 20½) in from beg, ending after a 2nd or 4th row.
Next row – K2, [k2 tog] 7 times, k2   *11 sts.*
Next row – Cast on 4(6, 8) sts, p across these sts, p11, cast on 14(16, 18) sts.   *29(33, 37) sts.*

Change to **4 mm** needles.
Next row – K2, [p1, k1] to last st, k1.
2nd row – K1, [p1, k1] to end. Rep these 2 rows for 7(9, 10) cm/3(3½, 4) in. Cast off *loosely* in rib.

LEFT SADDLE SHOULDER AND CUFF
Work as right section but reversing cast-on row for cuff.

BORDERS (2 pieces alike)
With **4 mm needles**, cast on 13 sts.
1st row – K2, p1, tw2, p1, k1, p1, tw2, p1, k2.
2nd row – K1, p1, k1, [p2, k1, p1, k1] twice.

Rep these 2 rows for approx 61(75, 88) cm/24(29½, 34½) in when slightly stretched, or until border fits up front, across one saddle and round to centre back of neck. Cast off.

TO MAKE UP
Omitting cuffs and borders, press, following pressing instructions on ball band. Join centre-back seam. Leaving 24(28, 32) centre sts free at top of back for neck, sew saddles in position to top of back and fronts. Stitch cast-on groups of sts on cuffs to corresponding sections of side edges of main part, slightly easing in main part. Join cuffs and side seams as far as shapings. Sew on borders, joining ends at back of neck. Work 2 rows of double crochet all round lower edges taking care *not* to stretch lower edges. Press seams and border.

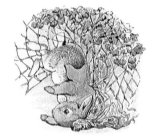

It was a blue jacket with brass buttons, quite new.
THE TALE OF PETER RABBIT

MEASUREMENTS

To fit bust	81	86	91	97	102	cm
	32	34	36	38	40	in
Length from	70	71	71	72	72	cm
shoulder	27½	28	28	28½	28½	in
Sleeve seam	47	47	47	47	47	cm
	18½	18½	18½	18½	18½	in

MATERIALS

Jaeger Monte Cristo, 50 g balls

17	17	18	18	19

A pair each 4 mm/No 8 and 3¼ mm/No 10 needles. A cable needle. 10 buttons.

TENSION

21 sts and 28 rows to 10 cm/4 in over main patt (on sleeves) on 4 mm/No 8 needles.

ABBREVIATIONS

K = knit; p = purl; sts = stitches; patt = pattern; inc = increase, increasing; dec = decrease, decreasing; beg = beginning; alt = alternate; rep = repeat; foll = following; sl = slip; psso = pass slipped st over; tog = together; tw2 = sl 1, k1, psso and k into back of it; CR4B = slip next 4 sts on cable needle to back of work, k5, now k4 from cable needle; MB = [k1, p1] twice all into front of next st thus making 4 sts out of 1, turn, sl 1, p2 tog, p1, turn, sl 1, k2 tog, psso; CR5F = slip next 5 sts on cable needle to front of work, k4, now k5 from cable needle; CB = slip next st on cable needle to back of work, k1, now p1 from cable needle; CF = slip next st on cable needle to front of work, p1, now k1 from cable needle; cm = centimetres; in = inches.

LEAF PANEL (worked over 39 sts)

1st row – CR4B, p6, MB, p3, k1, p3, MB, p6, CR5F.
2nd row – P9, k10, p1, k10, p9.
3rd row – K9, p10, k1, p10, k9.
4th and every foll alt row to 16th row – Work across 39 sts, knitting all k sts, and purling all p sts and MB sts.
5th row – K9, p8, MB, p1, k1, p1, MB, p8, k9.
7th row – K9, p8, CB, k1, CF, p8, k9.
9th row – K9, p7, CB, p1, k1, p1, CF, p7, k9.
11th row – K9, p6, [CB] twice, k1, [CF] twice, p6, k9.
13th row – K9, p5, [CB] twice, p1, k1, p1, [CF] twice, p5, k9.
15th row – CR4B, p4, [CB] 3 times, k1, [CF] 3 times, p4, CR5F.

16th row – P1, [k3, p1] twice, k4, [p1, k1] 3 times, p1, [k1, p1] 3 times, k4, [p1, k3] twice, p1.
17th row – [K1, p3] 3 times, [CB] 3 times, p1, k1, p1, [CF] 3 times, [p3, k1] 3 times.
18th and every foll alt row – Work across 39 sts, knitting all k sts, and purling all p sts.
19th row – [K1, p3] 3 times, p1, [CB] 3 times, k1, [CF] 3 times, p1, [p3, k1] 3 times.
21st row – [K1, p3] 3 times, p2, [CB] twice, p1, k1, p1, [CF] twice, p2, [p3, k1] 3 times.
23rd row – [K1, p3] 3 times, p3, [CB] twice, k1, [CF] twice, p3, [p3, k1] 3 times.
25th row – [K1, p3] 3 times, p4, CB, p1, k1, p1, CF, p4, [p3, k1] 3 times.
27th row – [K1, p3] 3 times, p5, CB, k1, CF, p5, [p3, k1] 3 times.
28th row – As 18th.
These 28 rows form panel.

RIGHT FRONT

With 3¼ mm needles, cast on 60(64, 68, 68, 72) sts.

1st row (right side) – K3, [p2, k2] to last st, k1.

2nd row – K1, [p2, k2] to last 3 sts, p2, k1. Work 17 more rows in rib.

Next row – Rib 17(21, 25, 19, 23), [inc in next st, rib 3] 6(5, 4, 7, 6) times, inc in next st, rib to end.   *67(70, 73, 76, 79) sts.*

Change to 4 mm needles and patt thus:

1st row – [K1, p1] 6(7, 8, 9, 10) times, tw2, p3, work 1st row of panel, p3(4, 3, 4, 3), tw2, [p1, k1] 3(3, 4, 4, 5) times.

2nd row – [P1, k1] 3(3, 4, 4, 5) times, p2, k3(4, 3, 4, 3), work 2nd row of panel, k3, p2, [k1, p1] to end.

3rd row – [P1, k1] 5(6, 7, 8, 9) times, p2, tw2, p3, work 3rd row of panel, p3(4, 3, 4, 3), tw2, p2, [k1, p1] to end.

4th row – [K1, p1] 2(2, 3, 3, 4) times, k2, p2, k3(4, 3, 4, 3), work 4th row of panel, k3, p2, k2, [p1, k1] to end.

5th to 28th rows – Rep 1st to 4th rows 6 times but working rows 5 to 28 of panel.

These 28 rows form patt. Continue in patt until work measures 63 cm/25 in from beg, ending at front edge.

Shape neck thus:

Cast off 8(9, 10, 10, 11) sts at beg of next row. Dec 1 st at neck edge on next 5 rows, then on the 2 foll alt rows.   *52(54, 56, 59, 61) sts.*

Work straight until front measures 70(71, 71, 72, 72) cm/ 27½(28, 28, 28½, 28½) in from beg, ending at side edge.

Shape shoulder thus:

Cast off 17(18, 19, 20, 20) sts at beg of next and foll alt row. Work 1 row. Cast off.

LEFT FRONT

Work to match right front but reverse patt rows, thus 1st row will be: [K1, p1] 3(3, 4, 4, 5) times, tw2, p3(4, 3, 4, 3), work 1st row of panel, p3, tw2, [p1, k1] 6(7, 8, 9, 10) times.

BACK

With 3¼ mm needles, cast on 120(128, 132, 140, 144) sts. Work 19 rows in rib as on right front.

Next row – Rib 21(25, 24, 28, 27), [inc in next st, rib 3] 7(6, 7, 6, 7) times, rib 21(29, 27, 35, 33), [inc in next st, rib 3] 7(6, 7, 6, 7) times, inc in next st, rib to end.   *135(141, 147, 153, 159) sts.*

Change to 4 mm needles and patt thus:

1st row – [K1, p1] 3(3, 4, 4, 5) times, tw2, p3(4, 3, 4, 3), work 1st row of panel, p3, tw2, p1, [k1, p1] 12(14, 16, 18, 20) times, tw2, p3, work 1st row of panel, p3(4, 3, 4, 3), tw2, [p1, k1] 3(3, 4, 4, 5) times.

2nd row – [P1, k1] 3(3, 4, 4, 5) times, p2, k3(4, 3, 4, 3), work 2nd row of panel, k3, p2, [k1, p1] 12(14, 16, 18, 20) times, k1, p2, k3, work 2nd row of panel, k3(4, 3, 4, 3), p2, [k1, p1] to end.

3rd row – [P1, k1] 2(2, 3, 3, 4) times, p2, tw2, p3(4, 3, 4, 3), work 3rd row of panel, p3, tw2, p2, [k1, p1] 11(13, 15, 17, 19) times, p1, tw2, p3, work 3rd row of panel, p3(4, 3, 4, 3), tw2, p2, [k1, p1] to end.

4th row – [K1, p1] 2(2, 3, 3, 4) times, k2, p2, k3(4, 3, 4, 3), work 4th row of panel, k3, p2, k2, [p1, k1] 11(13, 15, 17, 19) times, k1, p2, k3, work 4th row of panel, k3(4, 3, 4, 3), p2, k2, [p1, k1] to end.

5th to 28th rows – Rep 1st to 4th rows 6 times, but working rows 5 to 28 of panel.

These 28 rows form patt.

Keeping patt correct, cast on 30 sts at beg of next 2 rows. Working extra sts in main patt, work 42 rows on these 195(201, 207, 213, 219) sts.

Next 2 rows – Cast off 30 sts, patt to end.

Continue in patt until back measures same as fronts to shoulder shaping, ending after a wrong-side row.

Shape shoulders thus:

Cast off 17(18, 19, 20, 20) sts at beg of next 4 rows, then 18(18, 18, 19, 21) sts at beg of foll 2 rows. Slip final 31(33, 35, 35, 37) sts on a spare needle.

SLEEVES

With 3¼ mm needles, cast on 44(48, 48, 52, 56) sts. Work 31 rows in rib as on welt.

Next row – Rib 3(5, 1, 3, 5), [inc in next st, rib 1] 18(18, 22, 22, 22) times, inc in next st, rib to end.   *63(67, 71, 75, 79) sts.*

Change to 4 mm needles and main patt thus:

1st row – K1, [p1, k1] to end.

2nd and 3rd rows – P1, [k1, p1] to end.

4th row – As 1st.

Continue in patt as on these 4 rows, shaping sleeve by inc 1 st at each end of next and every foll 4th row until there are 107(111, 115, 119, 123) sts, taking extra sts into patt. Work straight until sleeve measures 47 cm/18½ in at centre. Cast off loosely.

NECKBAND

First join shoulders. **With 3¼ mm needles,** right side facing, k up 96(100, 104, 108, 112) sts evenly round neck including sts on spare needle. Beg with a 2nd row, work 22 rows in rib as on welt. Cast off.

BORDERS

First mark centre of each edge of neckband. **With 3¼ mm needles,** right side facing, k up 148 sts *evenly* spaced along right front edge to marker. Beg with a 2nd row, work 3 rows in rib as on welt.

Next row (buttonhole row) – Rib 6, [cast off 3 sts, rib 12 – including st on needle after cast-off] 9 times, cast off 3 sts, rib to end.

Next row – In rib, casting on 3 sts in each place where sts were cast off.

Rib 3 more rows. Cast off loosely in rib.

Work button border to match but omitting holes and commencing at neckband marker.

TO MAKE UP

Do not press. Stitch cast-off edges of sleeves to yoke, then join side and sleeve seams, lightly catching pocket linings of back to corresponding sections of fronts. Fold neckband in half to wrong side and hem in position all round. Sew on buttons.

LAKELAND
LANDSCAPE SWEATER

She pulled them off the wall, smacked them, and took them back to the house.

THE TALE OF TOM KITTEN

MEASUREMENTS

To fit bust	86–91	91–97	cm
	34–36	*36–38*	*in*
Length from shoulder	65	65	cm
	25½	*25½*	*in*
Sleeve length	47	47	cm
	18½	*18½*	*in*

MATERIALS

Lister Tahiti 5 Star Supreme, 50 g balls

Light Blue (M)	5	5
Green (A)	3	4

For the contrasts, use any of the Tahiti range in colours as follows: 2 balls (25 g) in Light Beige, 1 ball (25 g) each in Dark Grey (wall), Mid-Brown (gate), Mountain Grey (high mountains), White (lake), Light Pink (rhododendrons), Dark Pink (peonies), Bright Pink (foxgloves) and Lilac (iris).
A pair each 5 mm / No 6 and 4 mm / No 8 needles.

TENSION

16 sts and 22 rows to 10 cm / 4 in over st st on 5 mm / No 6 needles.

ABBREVIATIONS

K = knit; p = purl; sts = stitches; st st = stocking st; inc = increase, increasing; dec = decrease, decreasing; foll = following; beg = beginning; alt = alternate; rep = repeat; cm = centimetres; in = inches.

BACK

With 4 mm needles and A, cast on 69(73) sts.
1st row (right side) – K2, [p1, k1] to last st, k1.
2nd row – K1, [p1, k1] to end.
Rep these 2 rows for 9 cm / 3½ in, ending after a 1st row.
Next row – Rib 6(8), [inc in next st, rib 3] 14 times, inc in next st, rib to end.   *84(88) sts.***

Change to 5 mm needles and, beg with a k row, work 32 rows in st st.

Using small balls of yarn for each colour area where possible, otherwise carrying colour not in use *very loosely* over not more than 4 sts at a time, twisting yarns on wrong side when changing colour, continue in st st, **working the 55 rows from Chart 15A** (see page 102).
Continue in M only until work measures 65 cm / 25½ in at centre, ending after a p row.

Shape shoulders thus: Cast off 9(10) sts at beg of next 4 rows, then 10(9) sts at beg of foll 2 rows. Slip final 28(30) sts on a spare needle.

CHART 15A

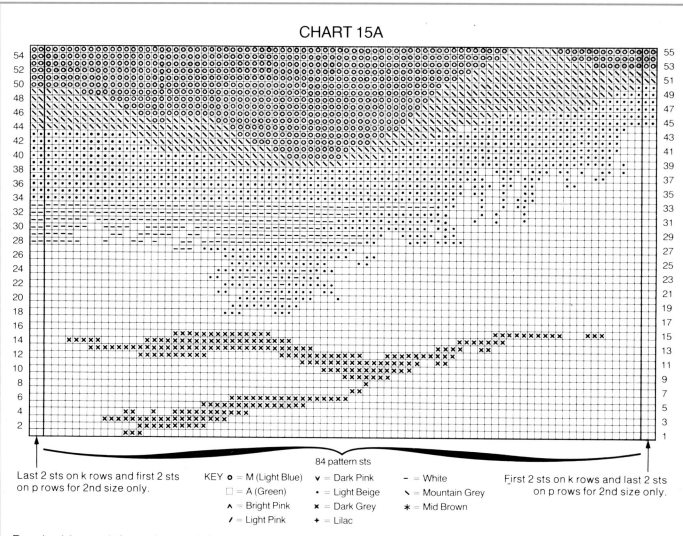

84 pattern sts

Last 2 sts on k rows and first 2 sts on p rows for 2nd size only.

KEY o = M (Light Blue)   v = Dark Pink   – = White
     □ = A (Green)   • = Light Beige   ╲ = Mountain Grey
     ∧ = Bright Pink   × = Dark Grey   * = Mid Brown
     ╱ = Light Pink   + = Lilac

First 2 sts on k rows and last 2 sts on p rows for 2nd size only.

Read odd rows k from right to left and even rows p from left to right, working 2 odd sts at each end of rows for 2nd size only as indicated.

FRONT

Work as back to **.

Change to 5 mm needles and, beg with a k row, work 2 rows in st st.
Now work the 85 rows from **Chart 15B**.
Continue in M only until work measures 56 cm/22 in from beg, ending after a p row.

Shape neck thus:
Next row – K34(35), turn.
Continue on this group. Dec 1 st at neck edge on next 3 rows, then on the 3 foll alt rows. *28(29) sts.*
Work straight until front measures same as back to shoulder shaping, ending at side edge.

Shape shoulder thus:
Cast off 9(10) sts at beg of next and foll alt row. Work 1 row. Cast off.

With right side facing, slip next 16(18) sts on a spare needle. Rejoin M and k 1 row. Complete as first side.

SLEEVES

With 4 mm needles and M, cast on 31(33) sts. Work in rib as on welt for 10 cm/4 in, ending after a 1st row.
Next row – Rib 1, [inc in each of next 2 sts, rib 1] 9(10) times, inc in next st, rib to end. *50(54) sts.*

Change to 5 mm needles and, beg with a k row, work in st st, shaping sleeve by inc 1 st at each end of 1st row, then on every foll 4th row until there are 72(76) sts, then on every foll 6th row until there are 82(86) sts.
Work straight until sleeve measures 47 cm/18½ in. Cast off loosely.

NECKBAND

First join left shoulder. **With 4 mm needles and M**, right side facing, k up 77(81) sts evenly round neck including sts on spare needles. Beg with a 2nd row, work 8 rows in rib as on welt. Cast off loosely in rib.

TO MAKE UP

Do not press. Join right shoulder and neckband. Stitch cast-off edges of sleeves in position to yoke. Join side and sleeve seams.

CHART 15B

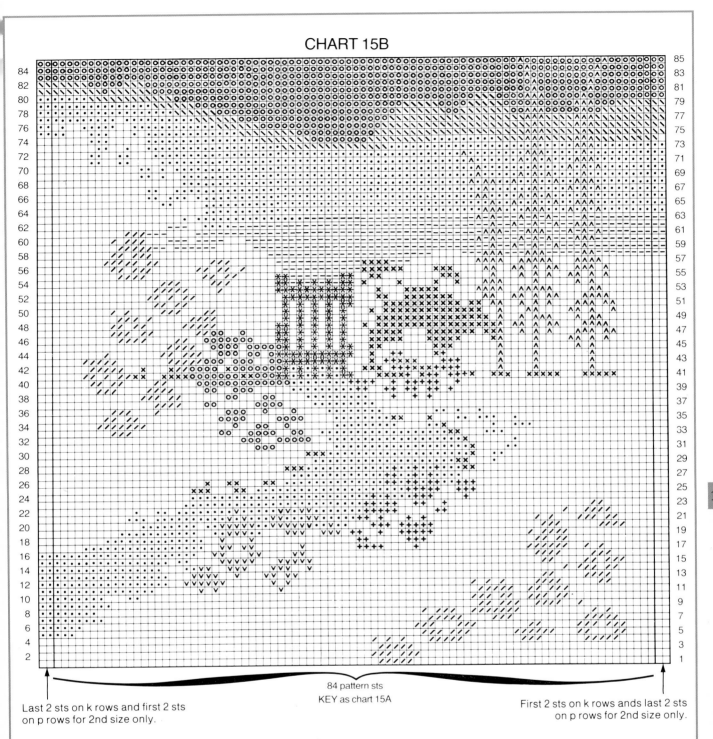

84 pattern sts
KEY as chart 15A

Last 2 sts on k rows and first 2 sts
on p rows for 2nd size only.

First 2 sts on k rows ands last 2 sts
on p rows for 2nd size only.

FOXGLOVE
SWEATER

He led the way to a very retired, dismal-looking house amongst the foxgloves.
THE TALE OF JEMIMA PUDDLE-DUCK

MEASUREMENTS

To fit bust	76	81	86	91	97	cm
	30	*32*	*34*	*36*	*38*	*in*
Length from	66	66	66	66	66	cm
shoulder	*26*	*26*	*26*	*26*	*26*	*in*
Sleeve seam	46	46	46	46	46	cm
	18	*18*	*18*	*18*	*18*	*in*

MATERIALS

Lister Libra Mosaics, 100 g balls

	5	5	5	6	6

A pair each 6½ mm/No 3 and 5 mm/No 6 needles. A cable needle. 3 buttons.

TENSION

14 sts and 20 rows to 10 cm/4 in over st st on 6½ mm/No 3 needles.

ABBREVIATIONS

K = knit; p = purl; sts = stitches; st st = stocking st; inc = increase, increasing; dec = decrease, decreasing; beg = beginning; alt = alternate; rep = repeat; foll = following; CF = slip next st on cable needle to front of work, p1, now k1 from cable needle; CB = slip next st on cable needle to back of work, k1, now p1 from cable needle; tog = together; cm = centimetres; in = inches.

STALK PANEL (worked over a basic 9 sts)

1st row (wrong side) – Inc knitways in next st, k3, p1, k3, inc knitways in next st. *11 sts.*
2nd row – CF, p3, k1, p3, CB.
3rd, 5th and 7th rows – Work across 11 sts knitting all k sts and purling all p sts.
4th row – P1, CF, p2, k1, p2, CB, p1.
6th row – P2, CF, p1, k1, p1, CB, p2.
8th row – P3, CF, k1, CB, p3.
9th row – K1, inc knitways in next st, k2, p3 tog, k2, inc in next st, k1.
10th to 25th rows – Rep 2nd to 9th rows twice.
26th row – P1, CF, p2, k1, p2, CB, p1.

27th and 29th rows – Work across 11 sts knitting all k sts and purling all p sts.
28th row – P2, CF, p1, k1, p1, CB, p2.
30th row – P3, CF, k1, CB, p3.
31st row – K2, inc knitways in next st, k1, p3 tog, k1, inc in next st, k2.
32nd to 36th rows – As 26th to 30th.
37th row – K4, p3 tog, k4. *9 sts.*
These 37 rows form panel.

FRONT

With 5 mm needles, cast on 61(65, 69, 73, 77) sts.
1st row (right side) – K2, [p1, k1] to last st, k1.
2nd row – K1, [p1, k1] to end.
Work 21 more rows in rib.
Next row – Rib 3(5, 7, 9, 11), [inc in next st, rib 3, inc in next st, rib 4] 6 times, inc in next st, rib to end. *74(78, 82, 86, 90) sts.*

Change to 6½ mm needles and work thus:
1st row (right side) – P21(22, 23, 24, 25), k1, p30(32, 34, 36, 38), k1, p21(22, 23, 24, 25).
2nd row – K21(22, 23, 24, 25), p1, k30(32; 34, 36, 38), p1, k21(22, 23, 24, 25).
Rep these 2 rows until work measures 36 cm/14 in from beg, ending after a 1st row.

Work Stalk panels thus:
1st row – K17(18, 19, 20, 21), work 1st row of panel, k22(24, 26, 28, 30), work 1st row of panel, k17(18, 19, 20, 21).
2nd row – P17(18, 19, 20, 21), work 2nd row of panel, p22(24, 26, 28, 30), work 2nd row of panel, p17(18, 19, 20, 21).
3rd to 37th rows – Rep 1st and 2nd rows 17 times, then 1st row again but working 3rd to 37th rows of panel.

Now working *all* sts in reverse st st, **shape neck** thus:
Next row – P29(31, 33, 35, 37), cast off next 16 sts (centre sts), p to end.
Continue on last group. Dec 1 st at neck edge on next 4 rows, then on every foll alt row until 21(23, 25, 27, 29) sts remain, then on every foll 4th row until 19(21, 23, 25, 27) sts remain.

Work straight until front measures 13 cm/5 in from top of panel, ending at side edge.

Shape shoulder thus:
Cast off 6(7, 8, 8, 9) sts at beg of next and foll alt row. Work 1 row. Cast off.

With wrong side facing, rejoin yarn to remaining sts and complete to match 1st half.

BACK
Work as front but noting that after welt has been worked, all sts should be worked in reverse st st.

SLEEVES
With 5 mm needles, cast on 31(31, 33, 33, 35) sts. Work 23 rows in rib as on welt.
Next row – Rib 8(6, 5, 4, 3), [inc once in each of next 2 sts, rib 1] 5(6, 7, 8, 9) times, inc in next st, rib to end.   *42(44, 48, 50, 54) sts.*

Change to 6½ mm needles and, beg with a k row for right side, work in st st, shaping sleeve by inc 1 st at each end of 3rd row, then every foll k row until there are 60(62, 66, 68, 72) sts, then on every foll 4th row until there are 80(82, 86, 88, 92) sts. Work straight until sleeve measures 46 cm/18 in from beg. Cast off loosely.

INSET
With 5 mm needles, cast on 159 sts.

1st row (wrong side) – K3, [p3, k3] to end.
2nd row – K1, p2, [k3, p3] to last 6 sts, k3, p2, k1.
3rd and 4th rows – As 1st and 2nd.
5th row – K3, [p1, p2 tog, k3] to end.   *133 sts.*
6th to 8th rows – Keeping ribs correct work 3 rows.
9th row – K3, [p2 tog, k3] to end.   *107 sts.*
10th to 12th rows – As 6th to 8th.
Next row – K1, k2 tog, [p1, k3 tog, p1, k1, k2 tog] to end.   *67 sts.*
Keeping ribs correct work 2 rows. Cast off in rib.

BELLS (make 30)
With 5 mm needles, cast on 8 sts loosely.
1st row (right side) – K.
2nd row – K1, p6, k1.
3rd row – K1, k2 tog, k2, k2 tog, k1.
4th row – K1, p4, k1.
5th row – [K2 tog] 3 times. Break yarn and run end through final 3 sts, draw up and fasten off.

TO MAKE UP
Do not press. Join shoulders. Placing side edges of inset edge-to-edge at centre front, sew inset evenly to neck edge of back and front. Join side edges of bells; sew 1 bell loosely to end of each stalk of panel, and 1 to each point where stalks join main stem. Stitch cast-off edges of sleeves to yoke. Join side and sleeve seams. Sew buttons to left-front edge of inset, then work a loop to correspond with each on right edge.

THE TAILOR OF GLOUCESTER
LADY'S FAIR-ISLE SWEATER AND RIBBED SKIRT

The waistcoat was worked with poppies and cornflowers.
THE TAILOR OF GLOUCESTER

MEASUREMENTS
SWEATER

Bust size	81–86	86–91	91–97	97–102	cm
	32–34	34–36	36–38	38–40	in
Length	63	65	66	67	cm
	25	25½	26	26½	in
Sleeve seam	43	43	43	43	cm
	17	17	17	17	in

SKIRT

Hip size	86–91	91–97	97–102	102–107	cm
	34–36	36–38	38–40	40–42	in
Length, excluding	75	75	75	75	cm
waist-band	29½	29½	29½	29½	in

MATERIALS
Patons Diploma DK, 50 g balls
SWEATER

Cream (M)	9	10	10	11
Green (C)	3	3	3	3
SKIRT	13	13	14	14

A large oddment each in Blue and Pink for Sweater embroidery.
A pair each 4 mm/No 8 and 3¼ mm/No 10 needles. Set of 3¼ mm/No 10 needles for Sweater neck. Length of elastic for Skirt.

TENSION
26 sts and 26 rows over patt and 22 sts and 30 rows over st st to 10 cm/4 in on 4 mm/No 8 needles.

ABBREVIATIONS
K = knit; p = purl; sts = stitches; st st = stocking st; patt = pattern; inc = increase, increasing; dec = decrease, decreasing; beg = beginning; foll = following; alt = alternate; rep = repeat; tog = together; cm = centimetres; in = inches; M = main shade (Cream); C = contrast shade (Green).

NB. When working from chart carry colour not in use loosely across back of work over not more than 5 sts at a time.

SWEATER

FRONT
With 3¼ mm needles and M, cast on 101(107, 113, 119) sts.
1st row (right side) – K2, [p1, k1] to last st, k1.
2nd row – K1, [p1, k1] to end.
Rep these 2 rows for 11 cm/4½ in, ending after a 1st row.
Next row – Rib 5(8, 11, 14), [inc in next st, rib 2] 30 times, inc in next st, rib to end. *132(138, 144, 150) sts.*

Change to 4 mm needles and, beg with a k row, work in st st, **working in patt from Chart 16A** (see page 109), reading odd rows k from right to left and even rows p from left to right, repeating the 22 patt sts 6 times across and working odd sts at each end of rows on 3 larger sizes as indicated until front measures 43 cm/17 in from beg, ending after a p row.

Keeping patt correct, **shape armholes** thus:
Cast off 10(11, 12, 13) sts at beg of next 2 rows. Dec 1 st at each end of next 7 rows, then on the 4 foll alt rows. *90(94, 98, 102) sts.*
Work straight **until** front measures **56(57, 57, 58)** cm/22(22½, 22½, 23) in from beg, ending after a p row.

Shape neck thus:
Next row – Patt 32(33, 34, 35), turn.
Continue on this group. Dec 1 st at neck edge on next 5 rows. *27(28, 29, 30) sts.*
Work straight until front measures 63(65, 66, 67) cm/25(25½, 26, 26½) in from beg, ending at armhole edge.

Shape shoulder thus:
Cast off 9(9, 10, 10) sts at beg of next and foll alt row. Work 1 row. Cast off.

With right side facing, slip centre 26(28, 30, 32) sts on a spare needle. Rejoin yarns. Patt 1 row. Complete as first side.

BACK
Omitting neck shaping, work as front to shoulder shaping, ending after a p row.

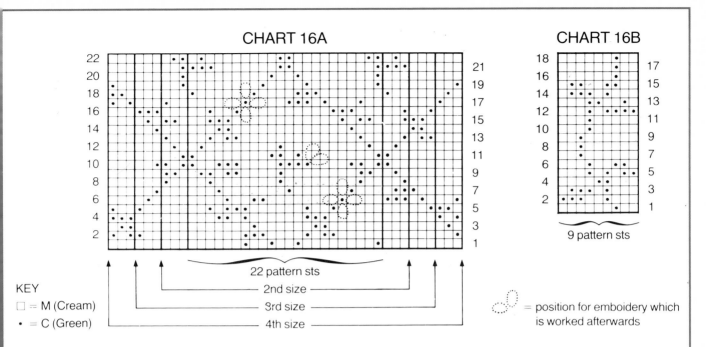

CHART 16A

22 21
20 19
18 17
16 15
14 13
12 11
10 9
8 7
6 5
4 3
2 1

CHART 16B

18 17
16 15
14 13
12 11
10 9
8 7
6 5
4 3
2 1

9 pattern sts

22 pattern sts
2nd size
3rd size
4th size

KEY
☐ = M (Cream)
• = C (Green)

⚘ = position for emboidery which
is worked afterwards

Shape shoulders thus:

Cast off 9(9, 10, 10) sts at beg of next 4 rows, then 9(10, 9, 10) sts at beg of next 2 rows. Slip final 36(38, 40, 42) sts on a spare needle.

SLEEVES

With 3¼ mm needles and M, cast on 43(45, 47, 49) sts. Work in rib as on front for 11 cm/4½ in, ending after a 1st row.
Next row – Rib 10(8, 3, 1), (inc in next st, rib 2) 7(9, 13, 15) times, inc in next st, rib to end. *51(55, 61, 65) sts.*

Change to 4 mm needles and patt, working from Chart 16B, thus:
1st row – K, 21(23, 26, 28)M, work 9 sts from 1st row of Chart 16B working from right to left, 21(23, 26, 28)M.
2nd row – P, 21(23, 26, 28)M, work 9 sts from 2nd row of Chart 16B working from left to right, 21(23, 26, 28)M.
3rd to 18th rows – Rep 1st and 2nd rows 8 times, but working 3rd to 18th rows of chart and inc 1 st at each end of 7th row foll, then on every foll 6th row.
Keeping chart correct as on these 18 rows, continue inc 1 st at each end of 3rd row foll, then on every foll 6th row to 63(67, 73, 77) sts, then on every foll 4th row to 85(89, 95, 99) sts.
Work straight until sleeve measures 43 cm/17 in, ending after a p row.

Shape top thus:

Cast off 10(11, 12, 13) sts at beg of next 2 rows. Dec 1 st at each end of every k row until 41(43, 43, 47) sts remain, then on every row until 31 sts remain for all sizes. Cast off.

NECKBAND

First join shoulders. **With set of 3¼ mm needles and M,** right side facing, k across back sts dec 3(5, 6, 7) sts evenly across, k up 21(21, 24, 24) sts evenly down left front neck, k across centre sts dec 3(3, 4, 5) sts evenly across, finally k up 21(21, 24, 24) sts evenly up right front neck. *98(100, 108, 110) sts.*
Work 17 rounds in k1, p1 rib. Cast off loosely.

TO MAKE UP

Embroider flowers as indicated on chart for front and back. Embroider flowers as desired on sleeves in pink and blue. Omitting ribbing, press, following pressing instructions on ball band. Join side and sleeve seams. Sew in sleeves. Fold neckband in half to wrong side and hem in position. Press seams.

SKIRT

FRONT AND BACK (2 pieces alike)

With 4 mm needles, cast on 183(193, 203, 213) sts.
1st row (right side) – K3, [p3, k1, p3, k3] to end.
2nd row – K3, [k3, p1, k3, p3] to last 10 sts, k3, p1, k6.
Rep these 2 rows 27 times more.
Next 2 rows – Cast off 3 sts, rib to end. *177(187, 197, 207) sts.*
Next row – [p3, k1, p3, k3] to last 7 sts, p3, k1, p3.
Next row – [K3, p1, k3, p3] to last 7 sts, k3, p1, k3.
Rep these 2 rows until work measures 58 cm/23 in from beg, ending after a wrong-side row.
Next row – [P1, p2 tog, k1, p1, p2 tog, k3] to last 7 sts, p1, p2 tog, k1, p2 tog, p1. *141(149, 157, 165) sts.*
Next row – [K2, p1, k2, p3] to last 5 sts, k2, p1, k2.
Next row – [P2, k1, p2, k3] to last 5 sts, p2, k1, p2.
Rep the last 2 rows until work measures 17 cm/6½ in from dec row, ending after a right-side row.
Next row – P2(3, 4, 5), [p2 tog, p1] 46(48, 50, 52) times, p to end. *95(101, 107, 113) sts.*
Change to 3¼ mm needles and work 8 rows in rib as on front of Sweater. Cast off *loosely* in rib.

TO MAKE UP

Press lightly following pressing instructions on ball band. Fold 3 sts at each edge on first 56 rows to wrong side and hem in position to 6th st from each edge. Join remainder of side seams. Cut elastic to fit waist; join in a ring; sew inside waist ribbing using herringbone stitch over elastic to form a casing. Press seams.

THE TAILOR OF GLOUCESTER
THREE KNITTED CUSHIONS

There was a snippeting of scissors, and snappeting of thread;
and little mouse voices sang loudly and gaily —
THE TAILOR OF GLOUCESTER

MEASUREMENTS
BOLSTER CUSHION   length 43 cm / 17 in
OBLONG CUSHION   40 × 60 cm / 15¾ × 23¾ in
SQUARE CUSHION   40 × 40 cm / 15¾ × 15¾ in

MATERIALS
Patons Diploma D K, 50 g balls
BOLSTER CUSHION, 2 balls in Cream (M) and 1 ball each in Green (C), Pink and Blue.
OBLONG CUSHION, 5 balls in Cream (M), 3 balls in Green (C) and 1 ball each in Pink and Blue.
SQUARE CUSHION, 4 balls in Cream (M) and 1 ball each in Green (C), Pink (A) and Blue (B).
A pair of 4 mm / No 8 needles. A piece of 122 cm / 48 in wide featherproof ticking for bolster cushion, also feather or synthetic filling
A 40 × 60 cm / 15¾ × 23¾ in cushion pad for oblong cushion.
A 40 × 40 cm / 15¾ × 15¾ in cushion pad for square cushion.

TENSION
26 sts and 26 rows to 10 cm / 4 in over patt.

ABBREVIATIONS
K = knit; p = purl; sts = stitches; st st = stocking st; patt = pattern; g st = garter st; tog = together; inc = increase, increasing; dec = decrease, decreasing; cm = centimetres; in = inches.

N B. When working from chart, carry colour not in use loosely across back of work over not more than 5 sts at a time. Read odd rows k from right to left and even rows p from left to right.

BOLSTER CUSHION

MAIN PART
With M, cast on 88 sts. Beg with a k row, **work from Chart 16A (see page 109)** in st st, commencing with 21st and 22nd rows, then repeating rows 1 to 22 until work measures 61 cm/24 in, ending after a 22nd row, noting that the 22 patt sts only should be repeated 4 times across. Cast off in M.

ENDS (2 pieces alike)
With Pink, cast on 132 sts. Beg with a k row, work 2 rows in st st.
Continue in st st, shaping thus:
1st row – K1, [k11, k2 tog] 10 times, k1.
2nd and every alternate row – P.
3rd row – K1, [k10, k2 tog] 10 times, k1.
5th row – K1, [k9, k2 tog] 10 times, k1.
Continue in this way, dec 10 sts on every following k row until 22 sts remain. P 1 row.
Next row – [k2 tog] 11 times. Break yarn; run end through 11 sts, draw up and fasten off securely.

TO MAKE UP
First make cushion pad. Allow 1 cm / ½ in turning for sewing of pad. Cut ticking into one rectangle 46 × 63 cm / 18 × 25 in and two 21 cm / 8½ in diameter circles. Join shorter ends of rectangle to form a tube. Sew one circle in position to one end of tube; now sew other circle half in position to other end. Stuff pad well with feather or synthetic filling, then join remaining section.
Embroider flowers as indicated on Chart 16A in Pink and Blue.
Join side edges of knitted ends. Press knitted pieces well, following pressing instructions on ball band. Join shorter ends of main part to form a tube. Sew one end in position to main part. Insert pad and sew other end in position. Make 2 tassels in Blue and sew one to centre of each end.

OBLONG CUSHION

Make 2 pieces alike, thus:
With M, cast on 106 sts. Beg with a k row, **work from Chart 16A** (page 109) in st st, repeating the 22 patt sts 4 times across and working the odd sts at each end of rows as given for 4th size on Chart 16A until work measures approx 60 cm/23¾ in from beg, ending after a 9th or 20th row of patt. Cast off in M.

TO MAKE UP
Embroider flowers as indicated on chart in Pink and Blue.

Press following pressing instructions on ball band.** Join 2 longer sides and 1 shorter side. Insert pad and join remaining seam, leaving small gap at one corner. Cut Pink into 4 lengths, each approx 635 cm / 250 in. Get a friend to hold one end while you hold the other. Each twist in the opposite direction until cord springs back on itself; knot ends together. Insert knotted end into gap left in seam and pin; then pin cord in position all round seam of cushion, allowing approx 11 cm / 4½ in for a loop at each corner. Carefully stitch in position; adjust final length at knotted end and close gap.

SQUARE CUSHION

Make 2 pieces alike. thus:
With M, cast on 82 sts *loosely*. Noting that 1st row will be right side, work in g st, working in stripes of 2 rows M, 2 rows A, 2 rows M, 2 rows B, 2 rows M, 2 rows C repeated throughout, *at the same time* dec 1 st at each end of every right-side row until 52 sts remain, thus ending after a dec row in M.
Next row – In M, k3, [make 1 by picking up and knitting into

back of horizontal strand lying before next st, k3, make 1, k4] 7 times.   *66 sts.*
Break A and B.
Change to st st and, beg with a k row, **work from Chart 16A**, commencing with 21st and 22nd rows and repeating the 22 patt sts only 3 times across. Now work rows 1 to 22 from chart 3 times.
Next row – In M, k3, [k2 tog, k2, k2 tog, k3] 7 times.   *52 sts.*
Next row – In M, k, inc 1 st at both ends.
Continue in g st working in stripes of 2 rows A, 2 rows M, 2 rows C, 2 rows M, 2 rows B, 2 rows M repeated throughout, *at the same time* inc 1 st at each end of every wrong-side row until there are 82 sts.
Cast off loosely in M.

Make 4 pieces alike, thus:
Work as first section from ** to **. K 1 row in M. Cast off loosely in M.

TO MAKE UP
Join shaped edges and cast-off edges of 4 g st sections to side edges of patt sections to form 2 squares. Make up as Oblong Cushion to **. Stitch 3 edges together. Insert pad and join remaining seam.

THE TAILOR OF GLOUCESTER
STITCHED RUG

*The little mice inside sprang to their feet,
and all began to shout in little twittering voices:
"No more twist! No more twist!"*
THE TAILOR OF GLOUCESTER

MEASUREMENTS
Finished rug size – 69 × 122 cm / 27 × 48 in

MATERIALS
Patons Turkey Rug Wool, 50 g balls

Shade		
	50	19 balls
	922	5 balls
	960	4 balls
	899	2 balls
	944	2 balls
	978	1 ball

N B. To ensure all shades are the same dye lot, it is advisable to purchase large amounts together.
Patons Brown check canvas 69 × 137 cm / 27 × 54 in
1 large bodkin needle

METHODS OF WORKING
Follow Chart 17 (see pages 114–15).

There are two alternative methods of working cross stitch: with the *row-by-row method* work a few half cross stitches, and then, starting with the last stitch, work back along the line thus completing the second half of each cross stitch. With the *stitch-by-stitch method* work each cross stitch individually.

It is essential when using either method to ensure that all stitches cross in the same direction, and it is important to maintain an even tension throughout the work.

The stitch-by-stitch method is preferable for working small areas of stitching like motifs where only a few stitches are likely to be worked in any one colour.

The row-by-row method is often used to cover large areas of fabric, such as the background of designs. It is quicker to work than the stitch-by-stitch method, and it is also easier to establish a regular rhythm with this method which helps to give the stitching an even tension.

ROW-BY-ROW METHOD
1. It is advisable to use lengths of wool no longer than 51 cm / 20 in to prevent wool wearing thin as it is worked.
2. To start stitching, leave a long horizontal thread under the row of canvas you are about to work. This avoids knots which may work through the canvas.
3. By bringing needle up at lower left-hand hole of the stitch to be worked and inserting it down through next diagonal hole, and repeating, half of each stitch is completed.
4. When all the half cross stitches over the intended area have been worked, bring the needle up through hole below and stitch back diagonally over the last stitch to complete the cross.
5. Working backwards, row by row, complete the second half of each cross stitch. Keep the tension of the stitches as even as possible for a neat appearance.
6. To fasten off thread on wrong side of work, slide needle through back of three or four stitches, pull thread through and cut. There is no need to backstitch.

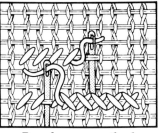

Row-by-row method

STITCH-BY-STITCH METHOD
1. An alternative method is to work each stitch individually. Work as steps 1 to 3 of row-by-row method, but do not repeat step 3.
2. To complete the stitch work back diagonally over the half cross worked previously and bring the needle up in the correct position for the next step. See Chart 18, Diagram 4. Fasten off as step 6 of row-by-row method.

STARTING AND FINISHING
Fold the first and last few inches of raw canvas under and press them flat; the stitches are then worked through the double canvas.

CHART 17

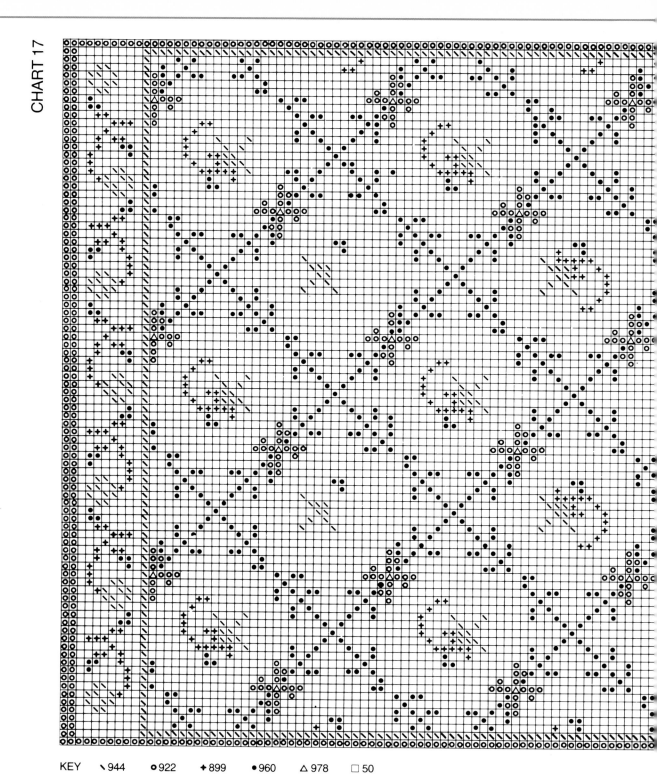

KEY   ＼944   ○922   ＋899   ●960   △978   □50

BINDING THE SELVEDGES

The selvedges are covered with corn stitch, which is a binding stitch and produces a very firm covering. With the wrong side facing, thread needle with shade 922, darn in end of wool and make a few upright sewing stitches as indicated on diagram. Now insert the needle in the first hole and bring it towards you, go over to the fourth hole, back to the second, forward to the fifth and so on.

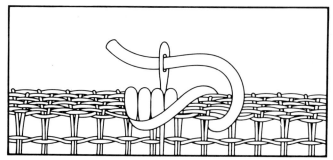

114

FINISHING OFF THE SHORT (FOLDED) ENDS

The short ends are bound with crossed oversewing stitches formed by working diagonally into every hole from left to right, then work a return row from right to left.

PRESSING STITCHED RUGS

Lay the finished rug on a padded surface, face down. Pull into shape, cover with a damp cloth and, using a hot iron, press all over including the sides.

CARE AND CLEANING OF STITCHED RUGS

To release dust, shake well. Vacuum both sides of rug. Dampen a cloth with liquid detergent and wipe carefully to clean the pile, but do not use much pressure or soak the rug. Dry by hanging on a line, away from direct sunlight, or laying flat.

Drycleaning is possible. Do not use a washing machine.

THE TAILOR OF GLOUCESTER
TAPESTRY FIRESCREEN

The stitches of those buttonholes were so small – so small – they looked as if they had been made by little mice!
THE TAILOR OF GLOUCESTER

MATERIALS
Anchor Tapisserie Wool (used for trammed gros point stitch throughout)
20 Powder Blue 0158
13 Kingfisher 0161
3 Smoke 0984
2 Beige 0376
1 Peat Brown 0360
1 Flesh Pink 0498

Anchor Stranded Cotton (used for cross stitch in 6 strands throughout)
10 Dusky Pink 0896
6 Forest Green 0216
5 Forest Green 0214
5 Dusky Pink 0894
5 Dusky Pink 0895
2 Cream 02
2 Sea Blue 0977
1 Sea Blue 0978

70 cm double-thread tapestry canvas, 10 holes to 2.5 cm, 69 cm wide.
Tapestry frame with 68 cm tapes.
Firescreen frame with backing board to fit (purchase on completion of embroidery).
Milward International Range tapestry needle No 18.

TO MAKE
N B. Follow Chart 18 opposite.
Mark the centre of canvas lengthwise and widthwise with a line of basting stitches. Mount canvas on frame with raw edges to tapes.

   Diagram 1 gives the complete centre design and the lower left-hand quarter of the border. The centre is indicated by black arrows which should coincide with the basting stitches. Each background square on Diagram 1 represents one intersection of double threads of canvas.

   Commence the design centrally and work following Diagram 1 and key for the embroidery. To complete the border work the lower right-hand quarter in reverse; then turn the canvas and work the remaining half of the border in the same way. If necessary, the embroidered canvas may be dampened, then pinned and stretched to the correct shape on a clean, dry board, using rustless drawing pins. Leave to dry naturally until the shape becomes permanent.

TO MAKE UP
Place embroidery centrally over the backing board, fold surplus canvas to the back and secure at top with pins into the edge of board. Pull firmly over the lower edge and pin in position. Repeat on side edges, pulling canvas until it lies taut on the board. Secure at the back by lacing from side to side both ways with strong thread. Remove pins and place in firescreen frame.

Diagram 2: Split Trammed Stitch. *Fig. 1*. The thread is brought through at the intersection where a pair of narrow vertical threads cross a pair of narrow horizontal threads. It is carried along the required distance (no longer than 13 cm) and passed through the canvas at a similar intersection of threads. *Fig. 2*. Bring the thread through 1 vertical thread to the left on the same line, piercing the stitch just made, thus forming a split stitch. Each trammed stitch must be placed in such a way that the stitches do not start or finish at the same pair of vertical threads.

Diagram 3: Trammed Gros Point Stitch. *Fig. 1*. Work a trammed stitch from left to right, then pull the needle through on the lower line; insert the needle diagonally into the upper line crossing the laid thread and 1 intersection of canvas threads (the point where a pair of narrow vertical threads cross a pair of narrow horizontal threads); bring the needle through on the lower line 2 canvas thread intersections to the left. Continue in this way to the end of the row. *Fig. 2* shows the reverse side of correctly worked gros point stitch, where the length of the stitches is greater than those on the front.

Diagram 4: Cross Stitch. *Fig. 1*. Bring the needle through at arrow, insert the needle at A over the intersection where a pair of narrow vertical threads cross a pair of narrow horizontal threads and bring out at B, forming a half cross. *Fig. 2*. Insert the needle at C and bring out again at B, completing the cross stitch. *Fig. 3* shows the completed cross stitch, with the needle shown in position for the next stitch when working crosses horizontally. It is important when working cross stitch to ensure that all the stitches cross in the same direction.

CHART 18

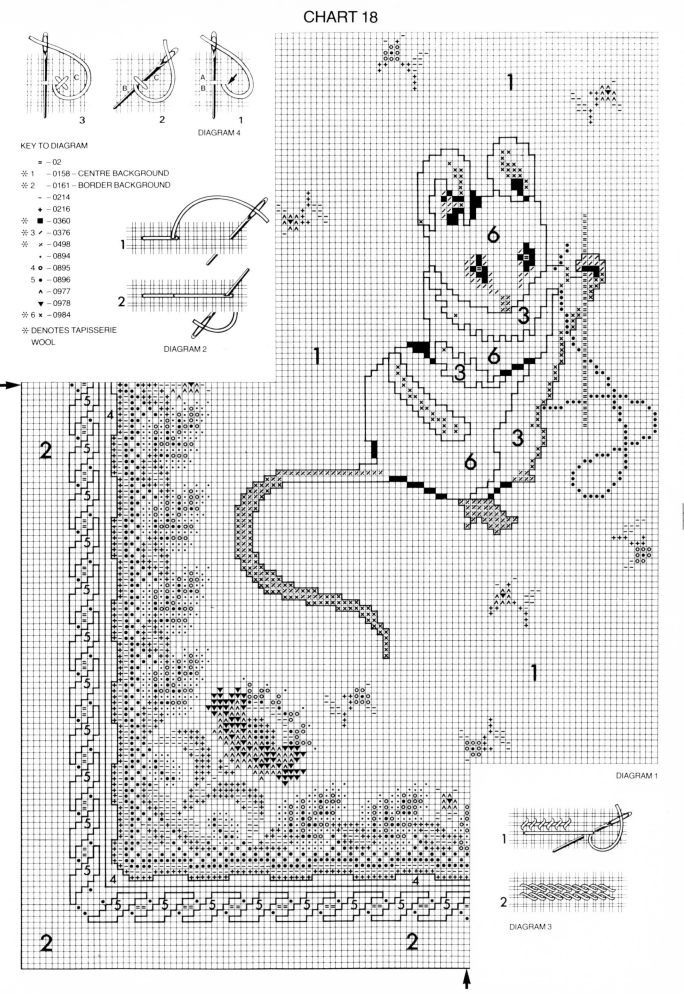

KEY TO DIAGRAM

= – 02
✳ 1 – 0158 – CENTRE BACKGROUND
✳ 2 – 0161 – BORDER BACKGROUND
  – – 0214
  + – 0216
✳ ■ – 0360
✳ 3 ✦ – 0376
✳ ✗ – 0498
  • – 0894
4 ○ – 0895
5 ● – 0896
  ∧ – 0977
  ▼ – 0978
✳ 6 ✗ – 0984

✳ DENOTES TAPISSERIE
  WOOL

DIAGRAM 4

DIAGRAM 2

DIAGRAM 1

DIAGRAM 3

TOMMY BROCK
FATHER AND SON SWEATERS

*Tommy Brock was a short bristly fat waddling person with a grin; he was
not nice in his habits. He ate wasp nests and frogs and worms.*

THE TALE OF MR. TOD

MEASUREMENTS

To fit	76	81	86	91	97	102	107	112 cm
chest	*30*	*32*	*34*	*36*	*38*	*40*	*42*	*44 in*
Length	49	54	60	65	67	69	69	69 cm
from	*19½*	*21½*	*23½*	*25½*	*26½*	*27*	*27*	*27 in*
shoulder								
Sleeve	37	42	46	48	48	48	48	48 cm
length	*14½*	*16½*	*18*	*19*	*19*	*19*	*19*	*19 in*

MATERIALS
For either version:
Sirdar Wash 'n' Wear Aran, 50 g balls

Grey (G)	11	12	13	15	17	18	19	20

1 ball (50 g) each Black (B) and White (W)
A pair each 5 mm / No 6 and 4 mm / No 8 needles. 2 buttons
for crossover neck version.

TENSION
18 sts and 27 rows to 10 cm/4 in over st st on 5 mm/No 6
needles.

ABBREVIATIONS
K = knit; p = purl; sts = stitches; st st = stocking st; inc =
increase, increasing; dec = decrease, decreasing; beg =
beginning; rep = repeat; cm = centimetres; in = inches;
G = Grey; B = Black; W = White.

POLO-NECK SWEATER

FRONT
With 4 mm needles and G, cast on 68(72, 76, 80, 84, 88, 92,
96) sts.
1st row (right side) – K3, [p2, k2] to last st, k1.
2nd row – K1, [p2, k2] to last 3 sts, p2, k1.
Work 20(20, 20, 24, 24, 24, 24, 24) more rows in rib, inc 8(8, 8,
8, 10, 10, 10, 10) sts evenly on last row.   *76(80, 84, 88, 94, 98,
102, 106) sts.*

Change to 5 mm needles and, beg with a k row, work 24(34,
44, 52, 58, 58, 58, 58) rows in st st.

Using small balls of yarn for each colour area where possible,
twisting yarns on wrong side when changing colour, otherwise carrying colour not in use *loosely* over not more than 3
sts at a time, continue in st st, **working from Chart 19** (see
page 120) thus:
1st row – K, 20(22, 24, 26, 29, 31, 33, 35)G, work 44 sts from
1st row of Chart 19 reading from right to left, 12(14, 16, 18,
21, 23, 25, 27)G.
2nd row – P, 12(14, 16, 18, 21, 23, 25, 27)G, work 2nd row of
Chart 19, reading from left to right, 20(22, 24, 26, 29, 31, 33,
35)G.
3rd to 34th rows – Rep 1st and 2nd rows 16 times but working
rows 3 to 34 of chart.**
Continue in G only and work straight until front measures
42(47, 51, 56, 57, 58, 58, 58) cm /16½(18½, 20, 22, 22½, 23, 23,
23) in from beg, ending after a p row.

Shape neck thus:
Next row – K30(32, 33, 35, 37, 38, 40, 42), turn.
Continue on this group. Dec 1 st at neck edge on next 4
rows.   *26(28, 29, 31, 33, 34, 36, 38) sts.*
Work 11(11, 13, 13, 17, 17, 17, 17) rows straight.

*** Work garter st band thus:
K, 2 rows B, 2 rows W, 2 rows B, 1 row G. Cast off *very loosely*
in G. *******

With right side facing, slip centre 16(16, 18, 18, 20, 22, 22, 22)
sts on to a spare needle. Rejoin G. K 1 row. Complete as first
side.

BACK
Omitting Tommy Brock and neck shaping, work as front up
to garter st band.
Work 5 more rows in G.

Shape shoulders by casting off 6(7, 7, 8, 8, 8, 9, 9) sts at beg of
next 6 rows, then 8(7, 8, 7, 9, 10, 9, 11) sts at beg of next 2
rows. Slip final 24(24, 26, 26, 28, 30, 30, 30) sts on to a spare
needle.

SLEEVES
With 4 mm needles and G, cast on 36(36, 40, 40, 40, 40, 44,

CHART 19

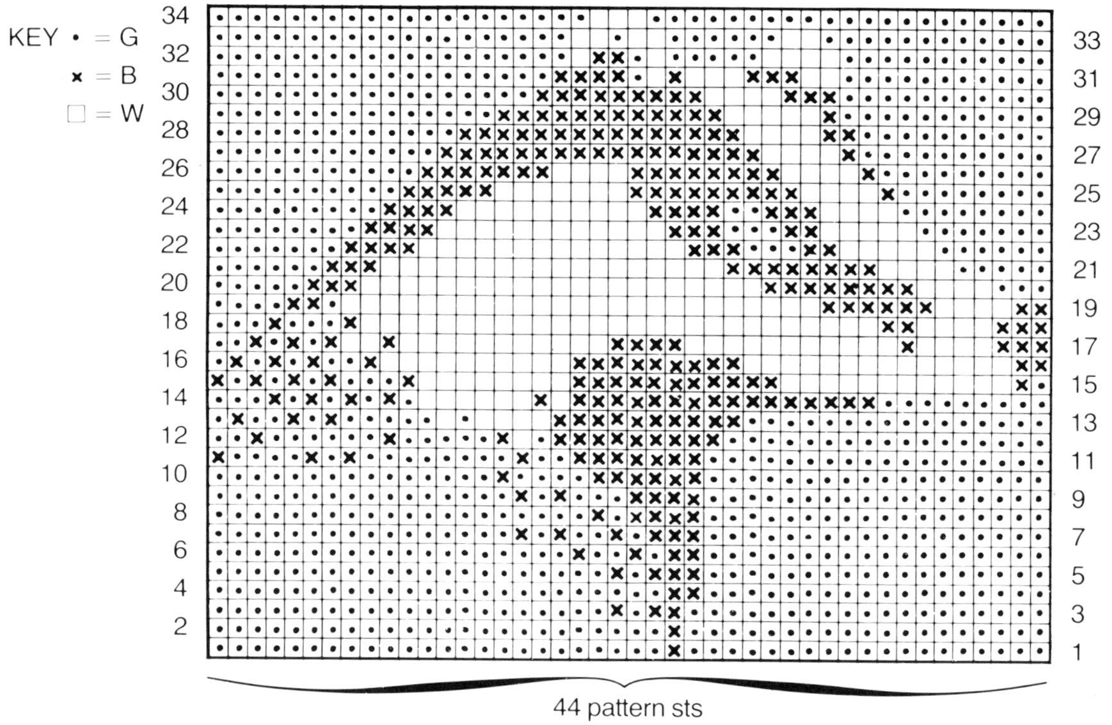

KEY • = G
✕ = B
☐ = W

Row numbers (left side, bottom to top): 2, 4, 6, 8, 10, 12, 14, 16, 18, 20, 22, 24, 26, 28, 30, 32, 34

Row numbers (right side, bottom to top): 1, 3, 5, 7, 9, 11, 13, 15, 17, 19, 21, 23, 25, 27, 29, 31, 33

44 pattern sts

44) sts. Work 22(22, 22, 26, 26, 26, 26, 26) rows in rib as on front, inc 6(8, 6, 8, 10, 12, 10, 12) sts evenly on last row.   *42(44, 46, 48, 50, 52, 54, 56) sts.*

Change to 5 mm needles and, beg with a k row, work in st st, inc 1 st at each end of 3rd row, then on every following 6th (8th, 8th, 8th, 4th, 4th, 4th 4th) row until there are 50(52, 58, 58, 56, 64, 72, 80) sts, then on every following 6th row for all sizes until there are 64(68, 72, 76, 82, 86, 90, 94) sts.

Work straight until sleeve measures 35(40, 44, 46, 46, 46, 46, 46) cm / 13¾(15¾, 17¼, 18¼, 18¼, 18¼, 18¼, 18¼) in from beg, ending after a p row.
Work as front from *** to ***.

POLO
First join left shoulder, slightly overlapping front shoulder over back. **With 4 mm needles and G**, right side facing, k across back sts, k up 15(15, 17, 17, 20, 20, 20, 20) sts evenly down left front neck, k across centre sts inc 6 sts evenly *on first 4 sizes only*, finally k up 15(15, 17, 17, 20, 20, 20, 20) sts evenly up right front neck.   *76(76, 84, 84, 88, 92, 92, 92) sts.*
Beg with a 1st row, work 42(44, 46, 50, 54, 56, 56, 56) rows in rib as on front. Cast off loosely in rib.

TO MAKE UP
Embroider eye in B. Omitting ribbing, press, following pressing instructions on ball band.** Join right shoulder and polo. Stitch cast-off edges of sleeves in position to yoke. Join side and sleeve seams. Press seams.

CROSSOVER NECK SWEATER

FRONT
Work as front of Polo-neck Sweater to **. Continue in G and work 6 rows.

Shape square neck thus:
Next row – K26(28, 29, 31, 33, 34, 36, 38), cast off centre 24(24, 26, 26, 28, 30, 30, 30) sts, k to end.
Continue on last group. Work straight for 16(17, 18, 19, 19, 21, 21, 21) cm / 6¼(6¾, 7¼, 7¾, 7¾, 8¼, 8¼, 8¼) in, ending after a p row.
Work as front of Polo-neck Sweater from *** to ***.

With wrong side facing, rejoin G. Complete as first side.

BACK AND SLEEVES
Work as Polo-neck Sweater, but casting off final back neck sts.

COLLAR
With 4 mm needles and G, cast on 36(36, 40, 40, 44, 48, 48, 48) sts. Work in rib as on front until strip fits all round front and back neck edges, omitting centre-front cast-off sts. Cast off firmly in rib.

TO MAKE UP
Make up as Polo-neck Sweater to **. Join shoulders, slightly overlapping front shoulders over back. Stitch cast-off edges of sleeves in position to yoke. Join side and sleeve seams. Overlapping left side over right, sew 2 short ends of collar neatly to centre-front neck, then sew side edge of collar to neck edge. Press seams. Work 2 buttonhole loops on lower edge of collar as in photograph, then sew on buttons to correspond.

OLD BROWN

SWEATER AND SLIPOVER FOR FATHER AND SON

Mr. Brown paid no attention whatever to Nutkin. He shut his eyes
obstinately and went to sleep.

THE TALE OF SQUIRREL NUTKIN

MEASUREMENTS

To fit chest	81	86	91	97	102	107 cm
	32	*34*	*36*	*38*	*40*	*42 in*
Length from shoulder	56	58	61	63	66	69 cm
(adjustable)	*22*	*23*	*24*	*25*	*26*	*27 in*
Sweater sleeve length	39	43	47	48	48	48 cm
(adjustable)	*15½*	*17*	*18½*	*19*	*19*	*19 in*

MATERIALS

SLIPOVER

Patons Beehive Chunky Twirl, 50 g balls

Oatmeal (L)	6	6	7	7	7	8

Patons Beehive Shetland Chunky, 1 ball (50 g) each in Dark Brown (D) and Mid Brown (M).
A pair each 6 mm / No 4 and 5 mm / No 6 needles.
An oddment of grey yarn for eyes and beak.

SWEATER

Patons Beehive Chunky Twirl, 50 g balls

Oatmeal (L)	10	10	10	11	11	12

Patons Beehive Shetland Chunky, 1 ball (50 g) each in Dark Brown (D) and Mid Brown (M).
A pair each 6 mm / No 4 and 5 mm / No 6 needles.
An oddment of grey yarn for eyes and beak.

TENSION

15 sts and 20 rows to 10 cm/4 in over st st on 6 mm/No 4 needles.

ABBREVIATIONS

K = knit; p = purl; sts = stitches; st st = stocking st; patt = pattern; inc = increase, increasing; dec = decrease, decreasing; beg = beginning; alt = alternate; foll = following; rep = repeat; cm = centimetres; in = inches; L = light (Oatmeal); D = dark (Dark Brown); M = medium (Mid Brown); 0 = no sts worked on this particular size.

SLIPOVER

FRONT

With 5 mm needles and D, cast on 61(65, 69, 73, 77, 81) sts.

1st row (right side) – K2, [p1, k1] to last st, k1.
2nd row – K1, [p1, k1] to end.
Working in stripes of 2 rows L, 2 rows M, 2 rows L, 2 rows D, continue in rib until work measures 9(9, 10, 10, 10, 10) cm/3½(3½, 4, 4, 4, 4) in from beg, ending after a 1st rib row.**

Next row – Using colour of last row, rib 0(2, 4, 6, 8, 10), [inc in next st, rib 4] 12 times, inc in next st, rib 0(2, 4, 6, 8, 10). *74(78, 82, 86, 90, 94) sts.*
Break D and M. Continue in L.

Change to 6 mm needles and, beg with a k row, work in st st until front measures 19(19, 20, 21, 24, 25) cm/7½(7½, 8, 8½, 9½ 10) in from beg, ending after a p row.

Using small balls of yarn for each colour area where possible, and twisting yarn on wrong side when changing colour, otherwise carrying colour not in use *loosely* over not more than 5 sts at a time, continue in st st, **working from Chart 20 (see page 122)** thus:
1st row – 21(23, 25, 27, 29, 31)L, work 1st row of chart, 21(23, 25, 27, 29, 31)L.
2nd to 44th rows – Rep 1st row 43 times but working rows 2 to 44 of Chart 20.

Break D and M. Continue in L and work until front measures 48(49, 52, 53, 56, 58) cm/19(19½, 20½, 21, 22, 23) in from beg, ending after a p row. (Adjust length here.)

Shape neck thus:
Next row – K30(32, 33, 34, 36, 37), turn.
Continue on this group. Dec 1 st at neck edge on next 3 rows. *27(29, 30, 31, 33, 34) sts.*
Work 6(8, 8, 10, 10, 10) rows straight.

Shape shoulder thus:
Cast off 9(10, 10, 10, 11, 11) sts at beg of next and foll alt row. Work 1 row. Cast off.

With right side facing, slip centre 14(14, 16, 18, 18, 20) sts on a spare needle. Rejoin L and k 1 row. Complete as first side, working 1 row more before shaping shoulder.

CHART 20

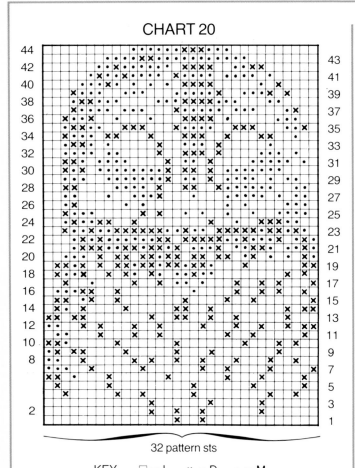

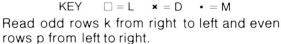

32 pattern sts

KEY □ = L **×** = D • = M

Read odd rows k from right to left and even rows p from left to right.

BACK

Omitting chart, work as front to neck shaping. Work 16(18, 18, 20, 20, 20) rows more.
(NB. Back is 6 rows longer than front to allow for saddle which sits to the front of garment).

Shape shoulders thus:
Cast off 9(10, 10, 10, 11, 11) sts at beg of next 4 rows, then 9(9, 10, 11, 11, 12) sts at beg of foll 2 rows. Slip final 20(20, 22, 24, 24, 26) sts on to a spare needle.

FRONT SADDLES (2 alike)

With 6 mm needles and L, cast on 6 sts.
1st and 2nd rows – In L, k.
3rd row – In D, k.
4th row – In D, p.
5th and 6th rows – In L, k.
7th and 8th rows – In M, as 3rd and 4th.
Rep these 8 rows until saddle fits across front shoulder, ending after 2 rows D, 2 rows L. Break yarns. Slip sts on a safety-pin and leave.

NECKBAND

First sew one long edge of each saddle neatly to front shoulder, placing safety-pin end at neck edge. Now sew other long edge of left saddle to back shoulder. **With 5 mm needles and L**, right side facing, k across sts of back and left saddle, k up 37(41, 43, 47, 47, 49) sts evenly round front neck including sts on spare needle, finally k across sts of right saddle. *69(73, 77, 83, 83, 87) sts.*
Beg with a 2nd row, work 6 rows in rib as on welt *but* working 1 row L, 2 rows M, 2 rows L, 1 row D. Cast off loosely in rib with D.

ARMHOLE BORDERS

First join right saddle to right back shoulder. Join neckband. Place a marker on each side edge approx 20(21, 23, 24, 25, 27) cm/8(8½, 9, 9½ 10, 10½) in down from *back* shoulder seam.
With 5 mm needles and L, right-side facing, k up 73(77, 81, 87, 91, 95) sts evenly between 1 set of markers. Work as neckband.

TO MAKE UP

Do not press. Embroider eyes and beak on Old Brown.******
Join side seams and edges of armhole borders.

SWEATER

BACK AND FRONT

Work as Slipover.

RIGHT SLEEVE

With 5 mm needles and D, cast on 27(29, 31, 31, 33, 33) sts.
Work as front of Slipover to ******, *but* ending after 2 rows L, 1 row M.
Next row – In M, rib 3(4, 3, 1, 4, 4), [inc in next st, rib 1] 10(10, 12, 14, 12, 12) times, inc in next st, rib to end. *38(40, 44, 46, 46, 46) sts.*

Change to 6 mm needles and st st, with centre stripe thus (NB. On 2-colour rows, carry L loosely over back of work over not more than 4 sts at a time, twisting yarn on wrong side when changing colour. Join in and break off D and L as required):
1st row – In L, k.
2nd row – In L, p19(20, 22, 23, 23, 23), k6, p13(14, 16, 17, 17, 17).

3rd row – K, 13(14, 16, 17, 17, 17)L, 6D, k to end in L.
4th row – P, using colours as on last row.
5th and 6th rows – As 1st and 2nd.
7th and 8th rows – Using M in place of D, as 3rd and 4th rows. These 8 rows form patt.

Continue in patt, shaping sleeve by inc 1 st at each end of next row, then on every foll 4th row until there are 52(54, 54, 60, 62, 62) sts, then on every foll 6th(6th, 6th, 6th, 4th, 4th) row until there are 58(62, 66, 70, 74, 76) sts, taking extra sts into L.
Work straight until sleeve measures 39(43, 47, 48, 48, 48) cm/15½(17, 18½, 19, 19, 19) in from beg, ending after a wrong-side row.
Next row – Cast off 23(25, 27, 29, 31, 32) sts, work to end.
Next row – Cast off 29(31, 33, 35, 37, 38) sts, work to end.

Continue in patt on remaining 6 sts until strip fits along front shoulder, ending after 2 rows D, 2 rows L. Break yarn. Slip sts on a safety-pin and leave.

LEFT SLEEVE
Work as right sleeve, reversing cast-off rows at top of sleeve and noting that 2nd row placing stripe will be: In L, p13(14, 16, 17, 17, 17), k6, p19(20, 22, 23, 23, 23).

NECKBAND
Work as Sweater.

TO MAKE UP
Make up as Sweater to **. Join right saddle to right back shoulder. Join neckband. Stitch sleeves in position to back and front. Join side and sleeve seams.

HELPFUL NOTES

TENSION

What does 'tension' mean? Why do I need to check my tension and how do I do this?

These two questions are frequently asked by knitters and the answers are simple: 'tension' means the number of stitches and rows, worked on a given size of needle, that are required to produce a piece of knitted fabric of a specified size. Every knitting pattern is based on a ratio of these. It is therefore vital to check that you knit to the stated tension – if your tension is not correct, the finished garment will not be the right size.

To check your tension, take the yarn and needles specified and cast on the number of stitches given in the tension paragraph plus 6 more. Work the stated number of rows plus 6 more. Slip the stitches off the needle. Place the sample on a flat surface and indicate with pins the number of stitches and rows stated in the tension paragraph. If your pinned square measures less than the size stated, your tension is too tight: try using a needle one size larger. If the square measures more than the size stated, your tension is too loose: try using a needle one size finer.

When knitting with a substitute yarn, it is not always possible to get the stitches *and* rows to the correct ratio. In this case always adjust the stitch tension (i.e. width) and adjust the length by working more or fewer rows than stated where possible.

HINTS FOR MOTIF KNITTING

You do not have to be an expert fair-isle knitter to work from a picture chart, but you do need a little patience initially. The satisfaction of producing a piece of picture knitting is immense and makes the effort well worth while.

It is worth the time to take a pair of needles and oddments of yarn and knit a trial piece from the chart you are going to knit, allowing about four extra stitches at each side of motif to be worked in the background colour. This will give you an idea of how many small balls of yarn in each colour you need to cut off ready before you start. By winding off a small ball (sometimes only a few centimetres) of yarn for each colour area, you will avoid a criss-cross effect at the back of the work, which might make the fabric bulky and distorted. Where only one or two stitches are worked in a given colour, these may be Swiss embroidered in the correct colour afterwards if desired, using the background colour for the actual knitted stitches.

Do not be tempted to use larger balls of yarn than required as these only drag on the work and can be difficult to disentangle. To estimate how much yarn to cut off for a given area allow, on average, approximately 18 cm/7 in for 10 stitches in double knitting, and 25 cm/10 in for 10 stitches in a chunky yarn; in addition you will need a little extra for joining in and breaking off. Do not knot new colours, but leave the end hanging on the wrong side; this can then be gently tightened afterwards to the correct tension and neatly darned in on the wrong side, taking care not to distort the right side of the fabric.

An alternative method of working a motif, or part of a motif, is to work it in Swiss embroidery afterwards, over the knitting. The embroidery looks just like knitting and is worked row by row and stitch by stitch following the chart to be worked.

SWISS EMBROIDERY

With a coarse tapestry needle threaded with the colour to be worked, begin at top right of motif.

1st row – Bring needle to right side of work through stitch below the first stitch to be worked. **Insert needle to right of stitch just above; bring it through again to right side of fabric on left of this stitch (*Fig. 1*). Insert needle in stitch below (where it first emerged) and bring up needle in next stitch to the left ** (*Fig. 2*). Work from ** to ** for as many times as required. After the last stitch, bring up needle through stitch below instead of through stitch to the left (*Fig. 3*).

Second row – Turn work round and work from right to left thus: Insert needle at bottom right of stitch below and bring it up again at left of same stitch. Insert needle through stitch above – that is, where it emerged to begin this 2nd row (*Fig. 4*).

After last stitch of 2nd row, bring up needle through stitch above and turn work. Continue repeating these 2 rows.

To work on a vertical line, begin at top. Make one stitch and bring up needle for next stitch through stitch below. Repeat for required number of vertical stitches.

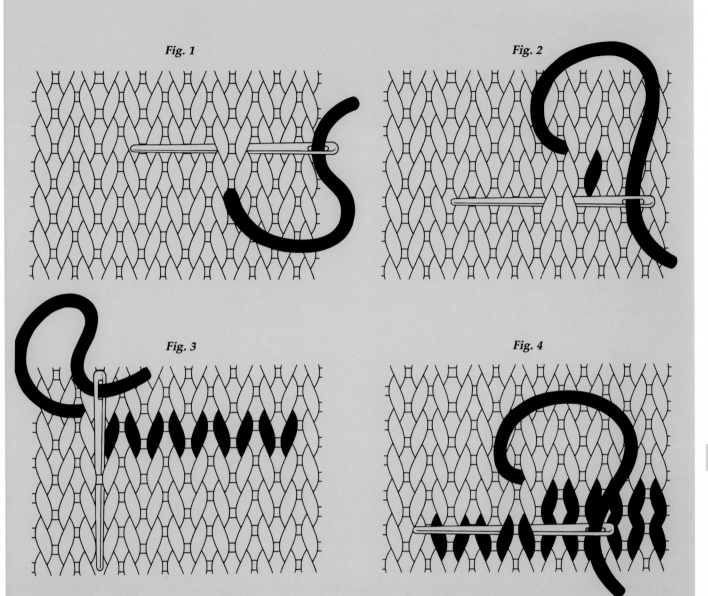

Fig. 1

Fig. 2

Fig. 3

Fig. 4

125

NEEDLE CONVERSION CHART

UK	USA	UK	USA
2 mm/14	00	5 mm/6	7
2¼ mm/13	0	5½ mm/5	8
2¾ mm/12	1	6 mm/4	9
3 mm/11	2	6½ mm/3	10
3¼ mm/10	3	7 mm/2	10½
3¾ mm/9	4	7½ mm/1	11
4 mm/8	5	8 mm/0	12
4½ mm/7	6		

YARN CONVERSION CHART

USING THE CHART

All the designs in this book were made up in the yarns given in the 'UK' column. Where these yarns are not readily available overseas, the nearest equivalent has been quoted for the different countries. Where no direct equivalent is known at the time of going to press, any reputable craft shop or yarn department will be happy to assist in selecting a suitable alternative to match the tension for any particular design. **It is imperative that you check your tension**, however, before commencing, and adjust your needle sizes accordingly if necessary to obtain the correct tension. For notes on tension see page 124.

Unless otherwise stated in the yarn conversion chart, use the needle sizes given in the instructions.

The quantities of yarn indicated in the instructions are an average requirement. When using a different yarn from that quoted in the instructions, the quantities required may well vary and we suggest that you take the advice of your yarn stockist on this.

If you experience difficulty in obtaining yarn, a useful list of addresses is given on page 128.

UK	USA	AUSTRALIA	CANADA	NEW ZEALAND	S AFRICA
Patons Beehive Chunky	Patons Beehive Chunky	Patons 12 ply Family	Patons Beehive Chunky	Patons Overlander	Patons Beehive Chunky
Patons Beehive Chunky Twirl	Patons Beehive Chunky Twirl	Patons 12 ply Family	Patons Beehive Chunky Twirl	Patons Overlander	Patons Beehive Chunky Twirl
Patons Clansman DK	Patons Beehive DK	Patons Totem 8 ply	Patons Beehive DK	Patons Totem 8 ply	Patons Beehive DK
Patons Beehive DK	Patons Beehive DK	Patons Totem 8 ply	Patons Beehive DK	Patons Totem 8 ply	Patons Beehive DK
Patons Diploma DK	Patons Beehive DK	Patons Totem 8 ply	Patons Beehive DK	Patons Totem 8 ply	Patons Diploma DK
Patons Baby Pure Wool 3 ply / Patons Fairytale 3 ply	Patons Baby 3 ply	Patons Babywool 3 ply	Patons Beehive Baby	Patons Babywool 3 ply	Patons Fairytale 3 ply
Patons Cotton Supersoft	Patons Cotton Soft/ Perle	Patons 8 ply Stonewash cotton	Patons Pearl Twist/Perle	Patons 8 ply Stonewash Cotton	Patons Cotton Soft
Patons Cotton Perle	Patons Cotton Perle	Patons 8 ply Perle	Patons Cotton Perle/Pearl Twist	Patons 8 ply Perle	Patons Cotton Perle
Patons Turkey Rug	—	—	—	Patons Turkey Rug	Patons Turkey Rug
Lister Tahiti 5 star Supreme/Tahiti Lights	Lister 5 star Supreme/Tahiti Lights	Lister 5 star Supreme/Tahiti Lights	Lister 5 star Supreme/Tahiti Lights	Patons Luxury Mohair on 4½ mm and 5½ mm needles	Lister 5 star Supreme/Tahiti Lights
Lister Libra Mosaics	Lister Libra Mosaics	Lister Libra Mosaics	Lister Libra Mosaics	Patons Savoy on 4½ mm and 5½ mm needles	Lister Libra Mosaics
Lister Bamboo Quartz	Lister Bamboo Quartz	Lister Venezia DK Cotton	Lister Venezia DK Cotton	Patons 8 ply Perle	Lister Richmond DK
Lister Motoravia DK	Lister Motoravia DK	Lister Motoravia DK	Lister Motoravia DK	Patons Totem 8 ply	Lister Richmond DK
Lister Machine Washable Aran	Lister Machine Washable Aran	Lister Machine Washable Aran	Lister Machine Washable Aran	Patons Capstan	Patons Capstan
Lister Shimmer Tweed	Lister Shimmer Tweed	Lister Shimmer Tweed	Lister Shimmer Tweed	Patons Luxury Mohair on 4½ mm and 5½ mm needles	Lister 5 star Supreme/Lister Tahiti Cotton
Lister Herdwick/Pure Wool Aran	Lister Pure Wool Aran	Lister Pure Wool Aran	Lister Pure Wool Aran	Patons Capstan	Lister Herdwick/Patons Capstan

UK	USA	AUSTRALIA	CANADA	NEW ZEALAND	S AFRICA
Lister Motoravia 4 ply	Lister Motoravia 4 ply	Lister Motoravia 4 ply	Lister Motoravia 4 ply	Patons Bluebell	Patons Beehive 4 ply
Hayfield Brushed Chunky	Hayfield Brushed Chunky	Hayfield Brushed Chunky	Hayfield Brushed Chunky	Hayfield Brushed Chunky	Hayfield Brushed Chunky
Hayfield Pretty Pastels DK	Hayfield Pretty Pastels DK	Hayfield Pretty Pastels DK	Hayfield Pretty Pastels DK	Hayfield Pretty Pastels DK	Hayfield Pretty Pastels DK
Hayfield Grampian DK	Hayfield Grampian DK	Sirdar Country Style DK	Hayfield Grampian DK	Hayfield Grampian DK	Hayfield Grampian DK
Hayfield Babykin DK	Hayfield Pretty Pastels DK	Hayfield Pretty Pastels DK/Pretty Whites DK	Hayfield Pretty Pastels DK/Pretty Whites DK	Hayfield Pretty Pastels DK/Pretty Whites DK	Hayfield Pretty Pastels DK/Pretty Whites DK
Wendy Family Choice DK	Wendy Family Choice DK	Patons Totem 8 ply on 3 mm and 3¾ mm needles	Wendy Family Choice DK	Wendy Family Choice DK	Patons Beehive DK on 3 mm and 3¾ mm needles
Wendy Peter Pan Darling DK	Wendy Peter Pan Darling DK	Wendy Peter Pan Darling DK	Wendy Peter Pan Darling DK	Wendy Peter Pan Darling DK	Patons Beehive DK on 3 mm and 3¾ mm needles
Wendy Shetland DK	Wendy Shetland DK	Patons Totem 8 ply on 3 mm and 3¾ mm needles	Wendy Shetland DK	Wendy Shetland DK	Patons Beehive DK on 3 mm and 3¾ mm needles
Richard Poppleton Plaza DK	Richard Poppleton Plaza DK	Patons Cotton Top on 3 mm and 3¼ mm needles	Richard Poppleton Plaza DK	Wendy Shetland DK	Patons Beehive DK on 3 mm and 3¾ mm needles
Richard Poppleton Emmerdale DK	Richard Poppleton Emmerdale DK	Patons 8 ply Perle on 3 mm and 3¼ mm needles	Richard Poppleton Emmerdale DK	Wendy Shetland DK	Robin Landscape DK on 3¾ mm needles
Robin Landscape DK	Robin Landscape DK	Robin Landscape DK	Robin Landscape DK	Patons Totem 8 ply	Robin Landscape DK
Robin Intrigue	Robin Intrigue	Emu Filigree	Robin Intrigue	Patons Mohair Amour	Patons Diana
Robin Bambino Raindrop DK	Robin Bambino Raindrop DK	Robin Bambino Raindrop DK	Robin Bambino Raindrop DK	Patons Child's Play/Patons Fairytale Misty DK	Robin Landscape DK
Sirdar Wash'n'wear Aran	Sirdar Wash'n'wear Aran	Sirdar Alpaca Cotton	Sirdar Wash'n'wear Aran	Wendy Family Choice Aran	Wendy Family Choice Aran
Sirdar Panorama DK	Sirdar Panorama DK	Sirdar Double Crepe	Sirdar Panorama DK	Sirdar Panorama DK	Hayfield Grampian DK on 3 mm and 3¾ mm needles
Argyll Fluffy Chunky	Robin Soft'n'Easy Chunky on USA 7 and 9 needles	Robin Soft'n'Easy Chunky on 5 mm and 6 mm needles	Argyll Fluffy Chunky	Patons Charm on 4½ mm and 5 mm needles	Patons Diana on 4½ mm and 5½ mm needles
Jaeger Monte Cristo	Jaeger Monte Cristo	Jaeger Monte Cristo/Patons Cotton Perle	Jaeger Monte Cristo/Patons Perle Twist	Patons 8 ply Perle	Patons Cotton Perle
Twilleys Capricorn Bulky	Lister Libra on 6½ mm needles	Twilleys Capricorn Bulky	Twilleys Capricorn Bulky	Patons Solo on 6½ mm needles	Twilleys Capricorn Bulky
Twilleys Galaxia 3	Lister Motoravia 4 ply	Twilleys San Remo 5 ply	Twilleys Galaxia 3	Patons Bluebell	Twilleys Galaxia 3

USEFUL ADDRESSES

If difficulty is experienced in obtaining the correct yarn, the following gives addresses where either head offices or agents/distributors for the various countries may be contacted.

No responsibility can be taken for any materials featured in this book which may be discontinued by manufacturers. Any reputable craft shop or department store will assist in choosing a satisfactory substitute.

UK	USA	AUSTRALIA	CANADA	NEW ZEALAND	S AFRICA
Patons/Jaeger PO Box Darlington Co. Durham DL1 1YQ	Susan Bates Inc. 212 Middlesex Avenue Chester Connecticut 06412	Coats Patons (Australia) Ltd PO Box 110 321–355 Ferntree Gully Road Mount Waverley Victoria 3149	Patons & Baldwins Canada Inc. 1001 Roselawn Avenue Toronto Ontario M6B 1B8	Coats Patons (New Zealand) Ltd Mohuia Crescent PO Box 50–140 Elsdon Porirua Wellington	Patons & Baldwins South Africa (Pty) Ltd PO Box 33 Randfontein 1760 Transvaal
Lister Handknitting George Lee & Sons Ltd Whiteoak Mills Westgate, Wakefield West Yorks WF2 9SF	Scotts Woollen Mills PO Box 1204 528 Jefferson Avenue Bristol PA 19007	B Willison & Co Pty Ltd PO Box 6 Mt Hawthorn WA 6016	Yarns Plus 120–5726 Burleigh CRSE Calgary Alberta T2H 12B	—	Mr Chris Rayner E. Brasch & Son 57 La Rochelle Road Trojan Johannesburg
Hayfield Textiles Ltd Glusburn Keighley West Yorks BD20 8QP	Shepherd Wools Inc 711 Johnson Avenue Blaine Washington 98230	Panda Yarns International (Pty) Ltd 17–27 Brunswick Road East Brunswick Victoria 3057	Craftsmen Distributors Inc. 4166 Halifax Street Burnaby British Columbia V5C 3X2	Alltex International 122 Victoria Street Christchurch	A & H Agencies 392 Commissioner Street Fairview Johannesburg
Wendy/Poppletons Wendy International Ltd PO Box 3 Guiseley Leeds LS20 9PD	White Buffalo Mills Ltd 6365 Kestrel Road Mississauga Ontario L5T 1S4 Canada	The Craft Warehouse 30 Guess Avenue Arncliffe NSW 2205	White Buffalo Mills Ltd 6365 Kestrel Road Mississauga Ontario L5T 1S4	Wendy Wools (NZ) Ltd PO Box 29107 Greenwoods Corner Auckland 3	Wendy Wools c/o Patons & Baldwins South Africa (Pty) Ltd PO Box 33 Randfontein 1760 Transvaal
Robin Wools Ltd Robin Mills Idle Bradford West Yorks BD10 9TE	The Plymouth Yarn Co. Inc. PO Box 28 500 Lafayette Street Bristol PA 19007	Karingal Vic/Tas Pty Ltd 359 Dorset Road Bayswater Victoria 3153	S.R. Kertzer Ltd 257 Adelaide Street West Toronto Ontario M5H 1Y1	—	—
Sirdar PLC Flanshaw Lane Alverthorpe Wakefield WF2 9ND West Yorks	Kendex Corporation 31332 Via Colinas 107 West Lake Village California 91362	Sirdar Australia (Pty) Ltd PO Box 110 Mt Waverley Victoria 3149	Diamond Yarn (Canada) Corp. 153 Bridgeland Unit 11 Toronto M6A 2Y6 Ontario	Alltex International 106 Parnell Road PO Box 2500 Auckland	—
Argyll Wools Ltd PO Box 15 Priestley Mills Pudsey West Yorks LS28 9LT	—	—	Estelle Designs & Sales Ltd 38 Continental Place Scarborough Ontario	—	—
H G Twilley Ltd Roman Mill Stamford Lincolnshire PE9 1BG	—	Panda Yarns Int. Ltd 17–27 Brunswick Road East Brunswick Victoria 3057	S.R. Kertzer Ltd 257 Adelaide Street West Toronto Ontario M5H 1Y1	—	F.W. Nyman & Co. (Pty) Ltd PO Box 292 Durban 4000
J & P Coats (UK) Ltd 39 Durham Street Glasgow G41 1BS	Susan Bates Inc. PO Box E Route 9A 212 Middlesex Avenue Chester Connecticut 06412	Coats Patons (Australia) Ltd PO Box 110 321–355 Ferntree Gully Road Mount Waverley Victoria 3149	J & P Coats (Canada) Inc. Station A PO Box 519 Montreal Quebec H3C 2T6	Coats Patons (New Zealand) Ltd PO Box 6149 Wellesley Street Auckland 1	J & P Coats (Pty) Ltd 4 Wol Street Homelake Extension Randfontein Transvaal

128